Modern Critical Views

Chinua Achebe
Henry Adams
Aeschylus
S. Y. Agnon
Edward Albee
Raphael Alberti
Louisa May Alcott
A. R. Ammons
Sherwood Anderson
Aristophanes
Matthew Arnold
Antonin Artaud
John Ashbery
Margaret Atwood
W. H. Auden
Jane Austen
Isaac Babel
Sir Francis Bacon
James Baldwin
Honoré de Balzac
John Barth
Donald Barthelme
Charles Baudelaire
Simone de Beauvoir
Samuel Beckett
Saul Bellow
Thomas Berger
John Berryman
The Bible
Elizabeth Bishop
William Blake
Giovanni Boccaccio
Heinrich Böll
Jorge Luis Borges
Elizabeth Bowen
Bertolt Brecht
The Brontës
Charles Brockden Brown
Sterling Brown
Robert Browning
Martin Buber
John Bunyan
Anthony Burgess
Kenneth Burke
Robert Burns
William Burroughs
George Gordon, Lord
  Byron
Pedro Calderón de la Barca
Italo Calvino
Albert Camus
Canadian Poetry: Modern
  and Contemporary
Canadian Poetry through
  E. J. Pratt
Thomas Carlyle
Alejo Carpentier
Lewis Carroll
Willa Cather
Louis-Ferdinand Céline
Miguel de Cervantes

Geoffrey Chaucer
John Cheever
Anton Chekhov
Kate Chopin
Chrétien de Troyes
Agatha Christie
Samuel Taylor Coleridge
Colette
William Congreve & the
  Restoration Dramatists
Joseph Conrad
Contemporary Poets
James Fenimore Cooper
Pierre Corneille
Julio Cortázar
Hart Crane
Stephen Crane
e. e. cummings
Dante
Robertson Davies
Daniel Defoe
Philip K. Dick
Charles Dickens
James Dickey
Emily Dickinson
Denis Diderot
Isak Dinesen
E. L. Doctorow
John Donne & the
  Seventeenth-Century
  Metaphysical Poets
John Dos Passos
Fyodor Dostoevsky
Frederick Douglass
Theodore Dreiser
John Dryden
W. E. B. Du Bois
Lawrence Durrell
George Eliot
T. S. Eliot
Elizabethan Dramatists
Ralph Ellison
Ralph Waldo Emerson
Euripides
William Faulkner
Henry Fielding
F. Scott Fitzgerald
Gustave Flaubert
E. M. Forster
John Fowles
Sigmund Freud
Robert Frost
Northrop Frye
Carlos Fuentes
William Gaddis
Federico García Lorca
Gabriel García Márquez
André Gide
W. S. Gilbert
Allen Ginsberg
J. W. von Goethe

Nikolai Gogol
William Golding
Oliver Goldsmith
Mary Gordon
Günther Grass
Robert Graves
Graham Greene
Thomas Hardy
Nathaniel Hawthorne
William Hazlitt
H. D.
Seamus Heaney
Lillian Hellman
Ernest Hemingway
Hermann Hesse
Geoffrey Hill
Friedrich Hölderlin
Homer
A. D. Hope
Gerard Manley Hopkins
Horace
A. E. Housman
William Dean Howells
Langston Hughes
Ted Hughes
Victor Hugo
Zora Neale Hurston
Aldous Huxley
Henrik Ibsen
Eugène Ionesco
Washington Irving
Henry James
Dr. Samuel Johnson and
  James Boswell
Ben Jonson
James Joyce
Carl Gustav Jung
Franz Kafka
Yasonari Kawabata
John Keats
Søren Kierkegaard
Rudyard Kipling
Melanie Klein
Heinrich von Kleist
Philip Larkin
D. H. Lawrence
John le Carré
Ursula K. Le Guin
Giacomo Leopardi
Doris Lessing
Sinclair Lewis
Jack London
Robert Lowell
Malcolm Lowry
Carson McCullers
Norman Mailer
Bernard Malamud
Stéphane Mallarmé
Sir Thomas Malory
André Malraux
Thomas Mann

Modern Critical Views

Modern Critical Views

SINCLAIR LEWIS

Edited and with an introduction by

Harold Bloom
Sterling Professor of the Humanities
Yale University

CHELSEA HOUSE PUBLISHERS
New York ◇ Philadelphia

© 1987 by Chelsea House Publishers,
a division of Main Line Book Co.

Introduction © 1987 by Harold Bloom

Printed and bound in the United States of America

10   9   8   7   6   5   4

∞ The paper used in this publication meets the minimum
requirements of the American National Standard for
Permanence of Paper for Printed Library Materials,
Z39.48-1984.

Library of Congress Cataloging-in-Publication Data
Sinclair Lewis
    (Modern critical views)
    Bibliography: p.
    Includes index.
    Summary: A collection of ten critical essays on the novels
of Sinclair Lewis, arranged in chronological order of original
publication
    1. Lewis, Sinclair, 1885–1951—Criticism and interpretation.
[1. Lewis, Sinclair, 1885–1951—Criticism and
interpretations.   2. American literature—History and
criticism]   I. Bloom, Harold.   II. Series.
PS3523.E94Z83 1987   813'.52   86-29912
ISBN 0-87754-628-2

Contents

Editor's Note

This book brings together the best criticism available upon the novels of Sinclair Lewis. The critical essays are reprinted here in the chronological order of their original publication. I am grateful to Vickie Forman for her work as a researcher.

My introduction centers upon *Arrowsmith*, including its share in Lewis's characteristic limitations, but also attempts to explain why it has become his most abiding work. H. L. Mencken begins the chronological sequence with his approving portrait of his fellow satirist as an exemplary American citizen, precisely because of his success in rendering the portrait of that grand imaginary American citizen, George F. Babbitt. T. K. Whipple, an admirable critic of Mencken's era, also writes about *Babbitt*, as part of an overview of Lewis, and arrives at the devastating verdict that: "Lewis is the most successful critic of American society because he is himself the best proof that his charges are just."

In another critical generation, Mark Schorer, Lewis's biographer, reaches much the same conclusion in a reading of *Elmer Gantry*, when he remarks that: "Sinclair Lewis is not unlike Elmer Gantry . . . *Elmer Gantry* reminds us that we continue to embrace as fervently as we deny this horror that at least in part we are."

Charles E. Rosenberg, examining *Arrowsmith*, ruefully sees Arrowsmith as the one Lewis hero whose spiritual potential is fulfilled, but at a certain societal and even personal cost. Lewis's satire is defended by Daniel R. Brown as an art of caricature, while the antithetical struggle with an American society he himself embodied is studied in Lewis's serials by Martin Bucco. The sociological imagination of Lewis is credited by Stephen S. Conroy with much of his earlier strength, but is then held responsible for the repetition and decline in the later novels.

Howell Daniels discovers more of the drama of dissociation in Lewis himself than in his novels. The representation of women in Lewis is studied by Nan Bauer Maglin, who finds him profoundly sympathetic to the struggle of women against the obstacles that are created for them by modern society.

This book ends with a reading of *Dodsworth* by Martin Light, who rightly finds in this neglected novel one of Lewis's strongest achievements, partly because the novel resolves, to some degree, the lifelong tension in Lewis, and his work, between romance and realism.

Introduction

It cannot be said, thirty-five years after his death, that Sinclair Lewis is forgotten or ignored, yet clearly his reputation has declined considerably. *Arrowsmith* (1925) is still a widely read novel, particularly among the young, but *Main Street* (1920) and *Babbitt* (1922) seem to be best known for their titles, while *Elmer Gantry* (1927) and *Dodsworth* (1929) are remembered in their movie versions. Rereading *Main Street* and *Elmer Gantry* has disappointed me, but *Babbitt* and *Dodsworth*, both good novels, deserve more readers than they now seem to have. Lewis is of very nearly no interest whatsoever to American literary critics of my own generation and younger, so that it seems likely his decline in renown will continue.

A Nobel prizewinner, like John Steinbeck, Lewis resembles Steinbeck only in that regard, and is now being eclipsed by Faulkner, Hemingway, Fitzgerald, and such older contemporaries as Cather and Dreiser. Lewis venerated Dickens, but the critical age when Lewis's achievement could be compared to that of Dickens or of Balzac is long ago over. Hamlin Garland, an actual precursor, is necessarily far more comparable to Lewis than Dickens or Balzac are. If, as Baudelaire may have remarked, every janitor in Balzac is a genius, then every genius in Lewis is something of a janitor. Essentially a satirist with a camera-eye, Lewis was a master neither of narrative nor of characterization. And his satire, curiously affectionate at its base (quite loving towards Babbitt), has no edge in the contemporary United States, where reality is frequently too outrageous for any literary satire to be possible.

Lewis has considerable historical interest, aside from the winning qualities of *Babbitt* and the surprising *Dodsworth*, but he is likely to survive because of his least characteristic, most idealistic novel, *Arrowsmith*. A morality tale, with a medical research scientist as hero, *Arrowsmith* has enough mythic force to compel a young reader to an idealism of her or his own. Critics have found in *Arrowsmith* Lewis's version of the idealism of Emerson and Thoreau, pitched lower in Lewis, who had no transcendental yearnings. The native strain in our literature that emanated out from Emerson into Whitman and Thoreau appears also in *Arrowsmith*, and helps account for the novel's continued relevance as American myth.

II

H. L. Mencken, who greatly admired *Arrowsmith*, upon expectedly ideological grounds, still caught the flaw in the hero, and the aesthetic virtue in the splendid villain, Pickerbaugh:

> Pickerbaugh exists everywhere, in almost every American town. He is the quack who flings himself melodramatically upon measles, chicken pox, whooping cough—the organizer of Health Weeks and author of prophylactic, Kiwanian slogans—the hero of clean-up campaigns—the scientific beau ideal of newspaper reporters, Y.M.C.A. secretaries, and the pastors of suburban churches. He has been leering at the novelists of America for years, and yet Lewis and De Kruif were the first to see and hail him. They have made an almost epic figure of him. He is the Babbitt of this book—far more charming than Arrowsmith himself, and far more real. Arrowsmith fails in one important particular: he is not typical, he is not a good American. I daresay that many a reader, following his struggles with the seekers for "practical" results, will sympathize frankly with the latter. After all, it is not American to prefer honor to honors; no man, pursuing that folly, could ever hope to be president of the United States. Pickerbaugh will cause no such lifting of eyebrows. Like Babbitt, he will be recognized instantly and enjoyed innocently. Within six weeks, I suspect, every health officer in America will be receiving letters denouncing him as a Pickerbaugh. Thus nature imitates art.

Mencken's irony has been denuded by time; Arrowsmith is indeed not typical, not a good American, not a persuasive representation of a person. Neither is anyone else in the novel a convincing mimesis of acutality; that was hardly Lewis's strength, which resided in satiric caricature. *Arrowsmith* ought to be more a satire than a novel, but unfortunately its hero is an idealized self-portrait of Sinclair Lewis. Idealization of science, and of the pure scientist—Arrowsmith and his mentor, Gottlieb—is what most dates the novel. I myself first read it in 1945, when I was a student at the Bronx

High School of Science, then an abominable institution of the highest and most narrow academic standards. As a nonscientist, I found myself surrounded by a swarm of hostile and aggressive fellow-students, most of whom have become successful Babbitts of medicine, physics, and related disciplines. *Arrowsmith*, with its naive exaltation of science as a pure quest for truth, had a kind of biblical status in that high school, and so I read it with subdued loathing. Rereading it now, I find a puzzled affection to be my principal reaction, but I doubt the aesthetic basis for my current attitude.

Though sadly dated, *Arrowsmith* is too eccentric a work to be judged a period piece. It is a romance, with allegorical overtones, but a romance in which everything is literalized, a romance of science, as it were, rather than a science fiction. Its hero, much battered, does not learn much; he simply becomes increasingly more abrupt and stubborn, and votes with his feet whenever marriages, institutions, and other societal forms begin to menace his pure quest for scientific research. In the romance's pastoral conclusion, Arrowsmith retreats to the woods, a Thoreau pursuing the exact mechanism of the action of quinine derivatives. Romance depends upon a curious blend of wholeheartedness and sophistication in its author, and Sinclair Lewis was not Edmund Spenser:

> His mathematics and physical chemistry were now as sound as Terry's, his indifference to publicity and to flowery hangings as great, his industry as fanatical, his ingenuity in devising new apparatus at least comparable, and his imagination far more swift. He had less ease but more passion. He hurled out hypotheses like sparks. He began, incredulously, to comprehend his freedom. He would yet determine the essential nature of phage; and as he became stronger and surer—and no doubt less human—he saw ahead of him innumerable inquiries into chemotherapy and immunity; enough adventures to keep him busy for decades.
>
> It seemed to him that this was the first spring he had ever seen and tasted. He learned to dive into the lake, though the first plunge was an agony of fiery cold. They fished before breakfast, they supped at a table under the oaks, they tramped twenty miles on end, they had bluejays and squirrels for interested neighbors; and when they had worked all night, they came out to find serene dawn lifting across the sleeping lake.
>
> Martin felt sun-soaked and deep of chest, and always he hummed.

I do not believe that this could sustain commentary, of any kind. It is competent romance writing, of the Boy's Own Book variety, but cries out for the corrected American version, as carried through by Nathanael West in *A Cool Million*, and in *Miss Lonelyhearts*. West's Shrike would be capable of annihilating salvation through back to nature and pure research, by promising: "You feel sun-soaked, and deep of chest, and always you hum."

    Arrowsmith was published in the same year as *The Great Gatsby* and *An American Tragedy*, which was hardly Lewis's fault, but now seems his lasting misfortune. *Babbitt* came out the same year as *Ulysses*, while *Dodsworth* confronted *The Sound and the Fury*. None of this is fair, but the agonistic element in literature is immemorial. *Arrowsmith* is memorable now because it is a monument to another American lost illusion, the idealism of pure science, or the search for a truth that could transcend the pragmatics of American existence. It is a fitting irony that the satirist Sinclair Lewis should be remembered now for this idealizing romance.

H. L. MENCKEN

Portrait of an American Citizen

The theory lately held in Greenwich Village that the merit and success of *Main Street* constituted a sort of double-headed accident, probably to be ascribed to a case of mistaken identity on the part of God—this theory blows up with a frightful roar toward the middle of *Babbitt*. The plain truth is, indeed, that *Babbitt* is at least twice as good a novel as *Main Street* was— that it avoids all the more obvious faults of that celebrated work, and shows a number of virtues that are quite new. It is better designed than *Main Street*; the action is more logical and coherent; there is more imagination in it and less bald journalism; above all, there is a better grip upon the characters. If Carol Kennicott, at one leap, became as real a figure to most literate Americans as Jane Addams or Nan Patterson; then George F. Babbitt should become as real as Jack Dempsey or Charlie Schwab. The fellow simply drips with human juices. Every one of his joints is movable in all directions. Real freckles are upon his neck and real sweat stands out upon his forehead. I have personally known him since my earliest days as a newspaper reporter, back in the last century. I have heard him make such speeches as Cicero never dreamed of at banquets of the Chamber of Commerce. I have seen him marching in parades. I have observed him advancing upon his Presbyterian tabernacle of a Sunday morning, his somewhat stoutish lady upon his arm. I have watched and heard him crank his Buick. I have noted the effect of alcohol upon him, both before and after Prohibition. And I have seen him when some convention of Good Fellows was in town, at his innocent

From *Sinclair Lewis: A Collection of Critical Essays*, edited by Mark Schorer. © 1962 by the Enoch Pratt Free Library.

sports in the parlors of brothels, grandly ordering wine at $10 a round and bidding the professor play "White Wings."

To me his saga, as Sinclair Lewis has set it down, is fiction only by a sort of courtesy. All the usual fittings of the prose fable seem to be absent. There is no plot whatever, and very little of the hocus-pocus commonly called development of character. Babbitt simply grows two years older as the tale unfolds; otherwise he doesn't change at all—any more than you or I have changed since 1920. Every customary device of the novelist is absent. When Babbitt, revolting against the irksome happiness of his home, takes to a series of low affairs with manicure girls, grass-widows, and ladies even more complaisant, nothing overt and melodramatic happens to him. He never meets his young son Teddy in a dubious cabaret; his wife never discovers incriminating correspondence in his pockets; no one tries to blackmail him; he is never present when a joint is raided. The worst punishment that falls upon him is that his old friends at the Athletic Club—cheats exactly like himself—gossip about him a bit. Even so, that gossip goes no further; Mrs. Babbitt does not hear it. When she accuses him of adultery, it is simply the formal accusation of a loving wife: she herself has absolutely no belief in it. Moreover, it does not cause Babbitt to break down, confess and promise to sin no more. Instead, he lies like a major-general, denounces his wife for her evil imagination, and returns forthwith to his carnalities. If, in the end, he abandons them, it is not because they torture his conscience, but because they seem likely to hurt his business. This prospect gives him pause, and the pause saves him. He is, beside, growing old. He is 48, and more than a little bald. A night out leaves his tongue coated in the morning. As the curtain falls upon him he is back upon the track of rectitude—a sound business man, a faithful Booster, an assiduous Elk, a trustworthy Presbyterian, a good husband, a loving father, a successful and unchallenged fraud.

Let me confess at once that this story has given me vast delight. I know the Babbitt type, I believe, as well as most; for twenty years I have devoted myself to the exploration of its peculiarities. Lewis depicts it with complete and absolute fidelity. There is irony in the picture; irony that is unflagging and unfailing, but nowhere is there any important departure from the essential truth. Babbitt has a great clownishness in him, but he never becomes a mere clown. In the midst of his most extravagant imbecilities he keeps both feet upon the ground. One not only sees him brilliantly; one also understands him; he is made plausible and natural. As an old professor of Babbittry I welcome him as an almost perfect specimen—a genuine museum piece. Every American city swarms with his brothers. They run things in the Republic, East, West, North, South. They are the originators and propagators of the national delusions—all, that is, save those which spring from the farms. They are the palladiums of 100% Americanism; the apostles of the Harding politics; the guardians of the Only True Christianity. They constitute the Chambers of Commerce, the Rotary Clubs, the Kiwanis Clubs, the Watch and Ward Societies, the Men and Religion Forward Movements, the Y. M. C. A. directorates, the Good Citizen Leagues. They are the advertisers who determine what is to go into the American newspapers and what is to stay out. They are the Leading Citizens, the speakers at banquets, the profiteers, the corruptors of politics, the supporters of evangelical Christianity, the peers of the realm. Babbitt is their archetype. He is no worse than most, and no better; he is the average American of the ruling minority in this hundred and forty-sixth year of the Republic. He is America incarnate, exuberant and exquisite. Study him well and you will know better what is the matter with the land we live in than you would know after plowing through a thousand such volumes as Walter Lippmann's *Public Opinion*. What Lippmann tried to do as a professor, laboriously and without imagination, Lewis has here done as an artist with a few vivid strokes. It is a very fine piece of work indeed.

Nor is all its merit in the central figure. It is not Babbitt that shines forth most gaudily, but the whole complex of Babbittry, Babbittism, Babbittismus. In brief, Babbitt is seen as no more than a single member of the society he lives in—a matter far more difficult to handle, obviously, than any mere character sketch. His every act is related to the phenomena of that society. It is not what he feels and aspires to that moves him primarily; it is what the folks about him will think of him. His politics is communal politics, mob politics, herd politics; his religion is a public rite wholly without subjective significance; his relations to his wife and his children are formalized and standarized; even his debaucheries are the orthodox debaucheries of a sound businessman. The salient thing about him, in truth, is his complete lack of originality—and that is precisely the salient mark of every American of his class. What he feels and thinks is what it is currently proper to feel and think. Only once, during the two years that we have him under view, does he venture upon an idea that is even remotely original—and that time the heresy almost ruins him. The lesson, you may be sure, is not lost upon him. If he lives, he will not offend again. No thought will ever get a lodgment in his mind, even in the wildest deliriums following bootleg gin, that will offer offense to the pruderies of Vergil Gunch, president of the Boosters' Club, or to those of old Mr. Eathorne, president of the First State Bank, or to those of the Rev. Dr. John Jennison Drew, pastor of the Chatham Road Presbyterian Church, or to those of Prof. Pumphrey, head of the Zenith

Business College, or even to those of Miss McGoun, the virtuous stenographer. He has been rolled through the mill. He emerges the very model
and pattern of a forward-looking, right-thinking Americano.

As I say, this *Babbitt* gives me great delight. It is shrewdly devised; it
is adeptly managed; it is well written. The details, as in *Main Street*, are
extraordinarily vivid—the speech of Babbitt before the Zenith Real Estate
Board, the meeting to consider ways and means of bulging the Chatham
Road Sunday-school, the annual convention of the real-estate men, Babbitt's
amour with the manicure-girl, the episode of Sir Gerald Doak, the warning
visit when Babbitt is suspected of Liberalism, the New Thought meeting,
the elopement of young Theodore Roosevelt Babbitt and Eunice Littlefield
at the end. In all these scenes there is more than mere humor; there is
searching truth. They reveal something; they mean something. I know of
no American novel that more accurately presents the real America. It is a
social document of a high order.

T. K. WHIPPLE

Glass Flowers, Waxworks,
and the Barnyard Symphonies
of Sinclair Lewis

Sinclair Lewis has said of himself: "He has only one illusion: that he is not a journalist and 'photographic realist' but a stylist whose chief concerns in writing are warmth and lucidity." Such illusions are not uncommon: the scientist who prides himself on his violin-playing, the statesman who would like to be known as a poet—most men would rather think of themselves as excelling in another activity than that in which they are eminent. Lewis's wish need not prevent us from adopting the general view of him, namely, that though he is a "photographic realist" and also, at times, something of a novelist or creative artist, yet after all he is primarily a satirist—unless indeed he is even more interesting as a product than as a critic of American society. Surely no one else serves so well as he to illustrate the relation between literature and a practical world: in such a world he has himself lived all his life, and such a world he portrays and holds up to ridicule and obloquy.

No small part of his effectiveness is due to the amazing skill with which he reproduces his world. His knack for mimicry is unsurpassed. He is a master of that species of art to which belong glass flowers, imitation fruit, Mme. Tussaud's waxworks, and barnyard symphonies, which aims at deceiving the spectator into thinking that the work in question is not an artificial product but the real thing. Of this art Zeuxis, who painted grapes so truly that birds came and pecked at them, is the most eminent practitioner; but Lewis's standard is often little short of the Zeuxine. Dyer's Drug Store, with its "greasy marble soda-fountain with an electric lamp of red and green and curdled-yellow mosaic," Babbitt's Dutch Colonial house in Floral Heights;

From *Spokesman: Modern Writers and American Life.* © 1928 by E. P. Dutton.

with its bathroom in which "the towel rack was a rod of clear glass set in nickel," and its bedroom in which were "the bureau with its great clear mirror, Mrs. Babbitt's dressing-table with toilet articles of almost solid silver, and the plain twin beds, between them a small table holding a standard electric bedside lamp, a glass of water, and a standard bedside book with colored illustrations"—thus thoroughly are the houses and stores and office buildings in Gopher Prairie and in Zenith represented for us down to the last minute particular. The inhabitants also are portrayed in corresponding fashion, as to their looks, their habits, their talk, their thoughts. Nothing could be more lifelike than Lewis's counterfeit world in all its accurate and unbearable detail. His novels are triumphant feats of memory and observation.

Not of course that they are not also much else besides; for one thing, his mimicry is all charged with hostile criticism and all edged with a satirical intent which little or nothing escapes. His is a world ruled by the desire of each individual for his own self-aggrandizement, and it shows the effects of such a rule plainly in its appearance. Viewed externally, Gopher Prairie is most conspicuous for its hit-or-miss ugliness, its lack of attraction for the eye or any other organ of sense. It looks as if its inhabitants were more or less permanently camping out, not as if they had built themselves a lasting habitation. It is dreary, haphazard, uncared for—only one degree better than the boom towns of the last century, thrown together by pioneers just to "do" for a while, and betraying essentially much the same spirit. Yet Gopher Prairie has passed the stage of pioneering; it is established and prosperous, but the people do not know what to do with their prosperity, as witness the interiors of their houses, with their shiny golden-oak furniture and their hideous carpets. Not a room in any of the dwellings nor a structure in the village—still less the village as a whole—was made with the design of its being well fitted to human life. All of it cries aloud an indifference to humane living. It is an accurate index to the attitude of the people.

Zenith, on the other hand, has attained a real beauty in its grouped towering skyscrapers, yet wholly by luck and accident, not purpose. And this beauty is only in the large; a closer inspection, though it shows comfort and luxury and even a kind of aesthetic striving, reveals this effort at beauty as spurious: from the Old English dining room of the Athletic Club to the sepia photographs on the living-room walls in Floral Heights, the taste for art is affected and unreal. The material showiness of Zenith is no improvement over the ugliness of Gopher Prairie, for it is conventional only, and the inhabitants find their truest pleasure in the accumulation of ingenious mechanical contrivances and conveniences. Zenith has arrived at the perfection of a mechanical luxury in which the only flaw is that it is altogether inhuman.

Life dehumanized by indifference or enmity to all human values—that is the keynote of both Gopher Prairie and Zenith. And nowhere does this animosity show itself more plainly than in hostility to truth and art. The creed of both towns is the philosophy of boosting, a hollow optimism and false cheeriness which leads directly to hypocrisy, as in making believe that business knavery is social service. Toward ideas likely to break this bubble of pretense the people are bitterly opposed; toward new ideas they are lazily contemptuous; toward other ideas they are apathetic. In both places, to be sure, there is a conventional gesture at the pursuit of culture; in Gopher Prairie the Thanatopsis Club listens to papers on the English Poets, and in Zenith a symphony orchestra is advocated as a means of civic advertisement. Yet intellectually both are cities of the dead, and in both the dead are resolved that no one shall live.

In *Main Street* and in *Babbitt*, the life of the mind is noticeable only because of the void left unfilled; in *Arrowsmith*, however, Lewis has devoted all of a long book to the tribulations of a seeker for truth in the United States, and his handling of the theme is masterly. The hero is a physician who becomes a bacteriologist. Before he finally takes refuge in the wilds of Vermont where he can pursue his researches undisturbed, he encounters all the difficulties which the United States puts in the way of a doctor and an investigator who would like to be honest; he struggles with the commercialism of the medical school, the quackery which thrives in the country, the politics and fraud of a Department of Public Health in a small city, the more refined commercialism of a metropolitan clinic, and the social and financial temptations of a great institute for research. He is offered every possible inducement to prostitute himself to an easy success—manifest, worldly success. Nor is he indifferent to the pressures which are brought to bear on him; on the contrary, being a scientist by instinct rather than by reasoned conviction, he wins out only in spite of himself. He would like to succeed, he has been contaminated by the success-worship with which he is surrounded, but he is unable to cope with an ineluctable honesty and stubborn drive in himself. In the end, he succumbs to his own integrity. When one reflects that of all thinkers the scientist is among us much the most favored, and that among scientists none is more encouraged than the medical man, one realizes that Lewis has wisely taken for his theme the form of intellectual life in which it appears at its best. Martin's troubles would have been still more serious had he been a chemist, economist, historian, philospher, or artist.

The intellectual life, however, is not the worst sufferer in the society Lewis deals with. The other humane activities fare no better; and of them all probably none is so debased as religion. In Gopher Prairie religion takes the form of repressive puritanism and prurient espionage. In Zenith, it is only one form of boosting, with a go-getter in the pulpit and the best of hustlers in the Sunday school. Nothing in Lewis's work reads so like outrageous burlesque as his account of Babbitt's campaign to increase attendance at the Sunday school; yet no student of Mencken's *Americana* will dare to say that Lewis has not been scrupulously truthful. There is nothing unusual in "the good time the Sacred Trinity class of girls had at their wieniewurst party," nor in the publicity given "the value of the Prayer-life in attaining financial success." If Lewis goes so far as to fall into low farce, it is only in pursuit of absolute verisimilitude.

No doubt every detail of *Elmer Gantry* is faithfully accurate, and one ought to be grateful to Lewis for so detailed a clinical report on the morbid symptoms which attack religion in a land where the religious spirit is dead. Nothing is omitted, no possible fraud or quackery or hypocrisy or iniquity—nothing is missing but religion. And that perhaps is why one is less grateful than one ought to be. In the other books, there is always in some form or other some norm for comparison, some principle of protest—as there is in Carol Kennicott's aspirations, in Babbitt's sense of defeat, and most conspicuously in Arrowsmith's stubborn loyalty to science. The absence of relief—even comic relief—in *Elmer Gantry* may account for the fact that the book is so difficult to read and therefore, unfortunately, so much less effective as satire than its predecessors. It is too bad, for never has Lewis had so good a subject or such wealth of material. But perhaps I do *Elmer Gantry* an injustice; possibly the very qualities which make it inferior to *Arrowsmith* and the rest adapt it all the better to the audience at which it is aimed. However that may be, it can be studied with profit as a sociological survey—even if it cannot be read with pleasure as a work of literature—for as a report on the status of what passes as religion in most of the nation it has the virtue of completeness.

Furthermore, since Lewis's folk are not alive in senses, mind, or spirit, they could scarcely be expected to have a social life. They carry on, of course, a group existence, for solitude is terrifying to them. Yet when they have gathered together, they have nothing to say to one another. They tell stories, they talk about business and the weather and housekeeping and automobiles, they gossip endlessly and often maliciously. Their curiosity as to each other's doings, which is equalled only by their indifference to each other as persons, is not a friendly and welcoming curiosity. They do not really care to get acquainted with one another; they have, and are capable of having, no true personal relations. Sometimes they seek distraction in noise and artificial gaiety. Constantly they simulate goodfellowship and practise a forced and humorless jocularity, raucous and mechanical. Their sociability is ghastly as any lifeless imitation of a living thing must be ghastly. It is a dance of galvanized dead. Lewis's world is a social desert, and for the best of reasons, that it is a human desert. It is a social void because each of its members is personally a human emptiness.

The central vacuum at the core of these people is the secret which explains their manifestations. Having no substance in themselves, they are incapable of being genuine. They are not individual persons; they have never developed personality. A search for the real Babbitt reveals simply that there is no "real" Babbitt. There are several Babbitts who have never been integrated. And so the others: in their inner vacancy, they necessarily have no integrity, and therefore they are insecure and uncertain. Having no guide, no standard, in themselves, they are driven to adopting the standards and the ideas of the herd. Their only existence is in the pack—naturally they fight for their tribal taboos with the ferocity of savages. It is impossible that they should be anything but standardized and uniform, since the wellsprings of individuality have gone dry in them; and it is inevitable that their uneasiness should make them defend themselves by assuming a blatant self-satisfaction and a bloodthirsty intolerance. Being unsure, they are self-conscious and snobbish and cruel. Their ignorance leads to bigotry and to scornful and uncomfortable ridicule of what they do not understand—which is everything unlike themselves. The women are devoted to a conception derived from without, an inherited convention, of what constitutes gentility, refinement, "niceness." The men, after their own fashion, are equally fanatical in behalf of their own notions of respectability and propriety in behavior. To both men and women, life is a hollow shell of deportment, and of course they hate any one who threatens to crack the shell.

If in the land which Lewis depicts "life at its most passionate is but a low-grade infection," the explanation is not far to seek. This society from the beginning has been developed under the dominance of one motive: the self-advancement of its separate members. The men are ruled mainly by the desire to get rich, the women by the desire to rise socially, but the two are ultimately the same. Both, in order to get up in the world, have denied themselves all other interests and experiences. They have starved themselves, until in the midst of the utmost material profusion they are dying of inanition. An unspoiled peasantry is rich in life in comparison with them, for they do not even live and grow like good vegetables, having cut themselves off from the source of nourishment. The instincts which cannot be entirely killed, such as sex, take on queer distorted forms among them. They are famine-sufferers who alienate sympathy by their own pride in their misshapenness and by their fierce determination that everyone else shall be as deformed as themselves. Were it not for their complacency and contemptuousness, they would be pathetic—and at times, in spite of everything, they are pathetic. For these folk, who enjoy ample opportunity to do whatever they like and who do not know what to do with themselves, suffer from an obscure but acute dissatisfaction. After all, the impluse to live cannot be altogether extinguished; it can only be frustrated. The victim, though self-sacrificed, realizes that he has missed something. Mrs. Babbitt turns for succor to vaporous forms of New Thought; Zilla Riesling finds an outlet in a degraded and vindictive religiosity.

But the spiritual malady which afflicts Zenith is most fully analyzed in the person of Babbitt himself. He feels vague longings which cannot be satisfied by the mechanical toys which are his "substitutes for joy and passion and wisdom," his "symbols of truth and beauty"; there is in him a wish for something beyond even electric cigar-lighters. When illness gives him an opportunity to stop and reflect, he is conscious that something is wrong:

> He lay on the sleeping-porch and watched the winter sun slide along the taut curtains, turning their ruddy khaki to pale blood red. The shadow of the draw-rope was dense black, in an enticing ripple on the canvas. He found pleasure in the curve of it, sighed as the fading light blurred it. He was conscious of life, and a little sad. With no Vergil Gunches before whom to set his face in resolute optimism, he beheld, and half admitted that he beheld, his way of life as incredibly mechanical. Mechanical business— a brisk selling of badly built houses. Mechanical religion—a dry, hard church, shut off from the real life of the streets, inhumanly respectable as a top-hat. Mechanical golf and dinner-parties and bridge and conversation. Save with Paul Riesling, mechanical friendships—back-slapping and jocular, never daring to essay the test of quietness.
>
> It was coming to him that perhaps all life as he knew it and vigorously practiced it was futile; that heaven as portrayed by the Reverend Dr. John Jennison Drew was neither very probable nor very interesting; that he hadn't much pleasure out of making money; that it was of doubtful worth to rear children merely that

they might rear children who would rear children. What was it all about? What did he want?

Babbitt seeks relief in philandering and in drink, but finds hardly even a momentary distraction. He attempts a timid excursion into liberal thought—liberal for Zenith—but is frightened and cajoled back into orthodoxy. His only real happiness he finds in a few days' vacation with Paul Riesling in the Maine woods.

The discontent which is common among the pillars of Zenith's civilization flares at times into open rebellion among the less compliant members of the community. Paul Riesling, who should have been a violinist and who instead went into the tar-roofing business, is in complete revolt and is finally reduced to committing murder. Chump Frink, the syndicated poet, gets drunk and lets out the secret of his thwarted aspirations. Gopher Prairie likewise has many malcontents: Guy Pollock, the lawyer, the one civilized man in the town, a victim to what he calls "the village virus"; Raymie Wutherspoon, the shoe clerk, with his futile yearnings toward sweetness and light; Erik Valborg, the tailor's assistant, with a spark, but only a spark, of the true fire. Not the least tragic aspect of both city and country is the effect they have on such as these, denying them possibility of healthy growth, condemning them to ineffectuality if not to freakishness. The rebels are as badly off as the conformists; for in a society in which the bread of life is nowhere to be found, the few isolated seekers for it are in a hopeless situation, foredoomed to being stunted and distorted both by lack of nourishment and by the hostility of their environment.

In short, in *Main Street*, *Babbit*, *Arrowsmith*, and *Elmer Gantry*, Sinclair Lewis has rendered in minute detail a vast panorama of an almost ideal practical society. To be sure, in my account of his work I have exaggerated the effect by omitting the shades and qualifications which are frequent in his books; nor does he himself analyze or explain the phenomena he depicts. Furthermore, Lewis himself, in spite of his fullness, has perforce selected and emphasized certain aspects of American life, so that his work cannot be taken as a complete portrait of the United States. His achievement is to have rendered more effectively than any one else several of the most conspicuous phases of our civilization. I hardly think that anyone will deny that the United States recognized itself in Lewis's portrait, which therefore, though unflattering, may be accepted as on the whole a good likeness. We are all certain to find our neighbors in the picture, and likely, somewhere or other, if we try, to find ourselves. Nor is the author himself absent. No special discernment is needed to detect a self-delineation in Lewis's novels, for after all the world he deals with is no more the world of Carol Kennicott, George F. Babbitt, Martin Arrowsmith, and Elmer Gantry than it is the world of Sinclair Lewis. He belongs to it as completely as do any of his creatures. He too was bred and born in the briar patch, and he has not escaped unscratched.

As a novelist Lewis has several peculiarities and limitations all of which point to a poverty of invention or imagination. One of his these, his fondness and aptitude for mimicry, has already been discussed. Closely allied to this trait is his extreme dependence on his own experience and on his power of observation. Another indication of the same weakness is the care with which he gets up his subjects, as he got up aviation for *The Trail of the Hawk*, or medicine and bacteriology for *Arrowsmith*. Furthermore, it is significant that his interest is in social types and classes rather than in individuals as human beings. With few exceptions, his treatment of his characters is external only; he confines himself largely to the socially representative surface, rarely exercising much insight or sympathy. He is above all a collector of specimens. May the explanation of this clinging to actuality and to externals not be that his imagination has failed to find adequate nutriment in his experience, especially in his social experience?

However that may be, of one thing there can be no doubt: that he has hated his environment, with a cordial and malignant hatred. That detestation has made him a satirist, and has barbed his satire and tipped it with venom. But his satire is no plainer a sign of his hatred than is his observation: he is as watchful as a wild animal on the lookout for its foes, or as a Red Indian in the enemy's country. His eye is always alert and keen for inconsistencies or weaknesses in his prey—and how quickly he pounces! Years of malicious scrutiny have gone to the making of his last four volumes. Such observation is but one sign of a defensive attitude. Undoubtedly, his hostility is only a reply to the hostility which he has had himself to encounter from his environment, such as every artist has to encounter in a practical society. But for the artist to adopt an answering unfriendliness is disastrous, because it prevents him from receiving and welcoming experience. From such a defensive shield, experience, which ought to be soaked up, rattles off like hail from a tin roof. I should judge that Lewis had been irritated rather than absorbed by his experience. His observation seems at the other extreme from realization; it seems vigilant and wary, whereas realization demands self-surrender and self-forgetfulness, and is possible only in friendly surroundings. If it be true that his imaginative power is somewhat lean and scanty, the fact would be in part accounted for by the enmity between him and his surroundings.

But to have evoked this enmity is not the only unfortunate effect which his environment has had on Lewis. Although he has changed not at all in essentials, some of his characteristics are disclosed more plainly in his early than in his later novels. *Our Mr. Wrenn, The Trail of the Hawk, The Job,* and *Free Air* assist materially toward an understanding of the author of *Main Street* and *Elmer Gantry.* In the former, for example, he betrays his defensive attitude in the extraordinary precautions he takes lest his readers misjudge him. He makes greater use of irony as a defensive weapon than any other writer I know of; he early made the discovery that if only he were ironical and showed that he knew better, he could be as romantic and sentimental and playful as he pleased. He writes as if always conscious of a hostile audience. He takes needless pains to make clear that he is more sophisticated than his characters, as if there were danger of our identifying him with them. He makes fun of their ingenuous enthusiasms, even when these enthusiasms have the best of causes. The result of it all is that he often seems unduly afraid of giving himself away.

In this respect he resembles his characters; nothing in them is more striking than their morbid self-consciousness. Only Will Kennicott and Leora are free from it. The others, especially those in the early books, are always wondering what people will think, always suspecting that they are the objects of observation and comment—and in Lewis's novels they are generally right. They are constantly posing and pretending, for the benefit even of waiters and elevator-boys. They do not dare to be natural; they are self-distrustful, uncertain, and insecure. They are self-analytical and self-contemptuous for their lack of sincerity; yet they continue to pose to themselves, adopting one attitude after another. That is to say, they conceive the object of life to be to pass themselves off as something they are not. This idea the author himself seems to share; he seems to think that the solution of all problems and difficulties is to find the one right pose, the one correct attitude.

Just as his people have no inner standards of their own, because they are not integral personalities, because they have not, in fact, developed any real personality at all, so Lewis himself shifts his point of view so often that finally we come to wonder whether he has any. One of the great advantages of *Arrowsmith* over its forerunners and its successor is that in it there seemed to emerge an almost established point of view. Otherwise, one would be inclined to call Lewis a man of multiple personality—save that all these personalities have a look of being assumed for effect. All the Lewises are disdainful of one another. When he has been romantic, he throws in a jibe at sentiment lest we think him sentimental; when he has been cynical, he grows tender lest he be thought hard; when he has been severe with a member of the Babbittry, he emphasizes the virtues of the common people and the absurdities of highbrows and social leaders. All his manifold attitudes, however, may be resolved into four: most conspicuously, he is the satirist who has flayed American society; least obviously, he is the artist whom one feels sure nature intended him to be; in addition, and above all in the early novels, he is a romanticist, and he is a philistine—these two bitterly abusive of each other. That is, besides his other reactions, he has tried to escape from his environment, and he has tried, with more success, to conform to it.

His romanticism is of two kinds. In the first place, there is in him much of the conventional romanticist and even of the sentimentalist. He has said of himself that he is "known publicly as a scolding corn-belt realist, but actually (as betrayed by the samite-clad, Tennyson-and-water verse which he wrote when he was in college) a yearner over what in private he probably calls 'quaint ivied cottages.' " This is the Lewis who flees from reality to fantasy, who sympathizes with Carol in her dislike of Gopher Prairie and in her longing for "a reed hut on fantastic piles above the mud of a jungle river," and who invents for Babbitt a dream of a fairy child playmate, "more romantic than scarlet pagodas by a silver sea." Then there is the second sort of romanticist, who has taken a tip from Arnold Bennett and gone in for the romance of the commonplace, who records the Swede farm-girl Bea's glamorous impressions of Main Street, who dilates on the excitement, adventure, and beauty of life in Zenith and who has no use for "Lloyd Mallam, the poet, owner of the Hafiz Book Shop," who wrote "a rondeau to show how diverting was life amid the feuds of medieval Florence, but how dull it was in so obvious a place as Zenith." To establishing the strangeness and beauty of humdrum life Lewis devoted his first four books; he undertakes to prove in *Our Mr. Wrenn* that a clerk's life in a Harlem flat is more romantic than travel in foreign lands, and in *The Job* that a stenographer is more romantic than Clytemnestra. This process is really no less an escape from reality than is the old-fashioned romance, for it consists, not in bringing out the essential quality and verity of ordinary life, but in casting a glamour over it and falsifying and sentimentalizing and prettifying it. Although romanticist the second is always highly contemptuous of romanticist the first, there is no essential difference between them.

Closely akin to the romanticist of the second sort is the Lewis who speaks as a man of the soil, one of the common herd, a Rotarian; he points out the essential goodness of small towns and their inhabitants and of boosters; he is homey and folksy, and strongly opposed to people whom he suspects of thinking that they are superior. This side of Lewis, plain enough in all his writing, is especially pronounced in the novels which preceded *Main*

Street; in the first of them, the account of Wrenn's marketing the Dixieland Inkwell, a glorification of the romance of business, is sheer Babbittry, and the account of Mrs. Arty's boarding-house, a glorification of folks who are just folks, is sheer Main-Streetism. In *Free Air*, an extravaganza on the theme of "Out Where the West Begins," the heroine learns during her transcontinental journey that "what had seemed rudeness in garage men and hotel clerks was often a resentful reflection of her own Eastern attitude that she was necessarily superior to a race she had been trained to call 'common people.' " According to Lewis the superiority is all the other way: people who have enjoyed the hereditary advantages of wealth, social position, and education are ridiculous and contemptible—unless, like Claire, they have the good luck to be regenerated by the Great West. His whole tendency in his first four stories is to bring a warm glow of self-satisfaction to the heart of the great American majority, to strengthen and entrench the folk of Zenith and of Gopher Prairie in their complacency and also in their intolerance of everyone unlike themselves. In short, he has not escaped contamination, but has partially conformed to his environment. One of the Lewises is a philistine.

Wonder has often been expressed at Lewis's popularity—that attacks such as his on American life and the American gods should meet a reception so enthusiastic. Yet I think his vogue is easily understood. For one thing, no doubt all the Zeniths enjoyed *Main Street* and all the Gopher Prairies *Babbitt*, and all who live on farms or in big cities liked both books. Moreover, Lewis caters to all tastes because he shares all points of view. For instance, I happened to see the play *Main Street* acted by a provincial stock company, and was amazed to find how readily the animus of the book had been shifted: a slight change had turned it into a traditional hick comedy—the rustics humorous but lovable and even admirable—and directed all the satire against Carol, Erik Valborg, and the other highbrows. Probably many readers took the novel so in the first place. In any case, whatever one's likes and dislikes, whether boosters, malcontents, romantics, radicals, social leaders, villagers, bohemians, or conventional people, one can find aid and comfort in the work of Sinclair Lewis.

Furthermore, Lewis's style must have contributed enormously to his success. It is of just the sort to please the people of whom he writes. His technique of raillery he has learned from Sam Clark and Vergil Gunch; he merely turns their type of wit and humor back upon themselves. All his satire is a long *tu quoque*. His crusade against the shortcomings of the clergy is conducted in the same spirit as Elmer Gantry's crusade against vice. His irony and sarcasm are of the cheap and showy variety popular on Main Street and in the Zenith Athletic Club:

> Babbitt's preparations for leaving the office to its feeble self during the hour and a half of his lunch-period were somewhat less elaborate than the plans for a general European war.

> the lithograph of a smirking young woman with cherry cheeks who proclaimed in the exalted poetry of advertising, "My tootsies never got hep to what pedal perfection was till I got a pair of clever classy Cleopatra Shoes."

Surely the point of these jibes would be plain even to Uncle Whittier or the Widow Bogart. Moreover, Lewis must think that his imitations or quotations of the speeches, advertisements, and conversation in *Babbitt* are amusing—that it is funny, that is, that the speakers should think themselves funny—and not merely dreary and faintly obscene. One comes finally to suspect, from his asperity, that not long ago the writer himself enjoyed such mispronunciations of *animiles, intellekschool, bacheldore, Heavings*. The reviewer who said that in *Elmer Gantry* Lewis had sent the preachers a comic valentine hit off Lewis's style to perfection. Lewis seems to aim at much the same stage of mental development as the movies, which is said to be the average age of fourteen. His manner is founded on the best uses of salesmanship, publicity, and advertising. It is heavily playful and vivacious, highly and crudely colored, brisk and snappy. He avails himself to all the stock tricks of a reporter to give a fillip to jaded attention. His people do not run, they "gallop"; instead of speaking, they "warble" or "gurgle" or "carol"; commonplace folk are "vanilla-flavored"; interior decorators are "daffodilic young men," "achingly well-dressed"; dancing becomes "the refined titillations of communal embracing." No wonder Lewis has sold satire to the nation—he has made it attractive with a coat of brilliant if inexpensive varnish. The excellence of his rare intervals of real writing is lost in the general glare.

For, though no one unaided could have guessed that Lewis thought himself "a stylist whose chief concerns in writing are warmth and lucidity," there are such intervals, and they serve to remind us from time to time of Lewis the artist, by no means insensible to beauty or devoid of the tragic sense of life. The account of Carl Ericson's boyhood in *The Trail of the Hawk* is full of poetry, and there are bits in the story of his *Wanderjahre* that make one wish Lewis had seen fit to develop the picaresque possibilites more fully. In *The Job*, the death of Una Golden's mother is powerfully felt and strongly written. And, although Carol Kennicott is mainly a medium and an object of satire, she is also a created character, as is Babbitt likewise. But Will Kennicott, who is little analyzed or dissected, is the best evidence before *Arrowsmith* that Lewis has the ability to create people. *Arrowsmith* itself, however, is the final proof of his creative power. Leora, Martin's first wife, is by general consent Lewis's masterpiece in the creation of character. Not only is she likable, but she is indubitably real; though she is portrayed casually and without effort, few other characters in American fiction equal her in absolute final reality. And Martin suffers only in comparison with Leora; although far more difficult than either Carol or Babbitt, he is more understandingly and more successfully portrayed. Yet even Leora interests Lewis less than his national portrait gallery of typical frauds and fakirs. He prefers to stay safely on the surface of social appearances. He shows little of Sherwood Anderson's hunger to delve into the lives of men and women.

The very mention of Anderson brings into sharp relief Lewis's limitations—his superficiality, his meretricious writing, his lack of passion and of thoughtfulness. If it were objected that the comparison has no point, Lewis being a satirist, I should reply that it is possible for a satirist to manifest penetration, strong feeling, and intellectual power, seeing that other satirists have obviously possessed these qualities. Yet I feel sure that Lewis has many unrealized capabilities. Underneath all the masks he puts on to rebuff or to placate the world, there seems to lurk a boyish artist, immature and shy and eager, full of fancy and sentiment, who has never grown up and ripened— denied his proper development, probably, by the necessity of manufacturing those protective masks. He is uncomfortable in the presence of other people, and feels at ease only with nature, on which he lavishes exquisite praise. The world would have none of him; so he will have none of the world. His world was a poor one at best, but he has denied himself even what little it might have offered. That is why he is still a boy, with a boy's insecurity and self-doubt hidden behind a forced rudeness and boldness.

In *Arrowsmith*, his seventh novel, Lewis showed signs of beginning to develop a point of view, an inner standard of measurement. But that it is too late now for him to abandon his assumed attitudes and adopt the position proper to the artist, with the self-reliance which can come only from a sense of there being a pivot or point of rest in himself, *Elmer Gantry* is sufficient evidence. To the present, at any rate, Lewis is significant mainly as a social rather than as a literary phenomenon. And though this fact heightens his immediate importance, it detracts ultimately even from his social importance. While many of his contemporaries, who have succeeded in maintaining their integrity unimpaired, impart to their readers an intenser realization of the world they live in, the net result of Lewis's work is not a truer apprehension or a deeper insight, but an increase in mutual dissatisfaction: he has made Americans more outspoken and more hostile critics of one another. But perhaps after all it is better so: Lewis's romanticism and philistinism and vulgarity of style make him powerful because they make him popular. The attack on American practicality needs its shock troops—could we afford to give up so effective a critic for a better writer? Perhaps it is worth spoiling an artist to have him take so salutary a revenge. Lewis is the most successful critic of American society because he is himself the best proof that his charges are just.

MARK SCHORER

Sinclair Lewis and the Method of Half-Truths

Let us begin with a pair of quotations that are concerned with the conception of the novel as a social instrument. The two conceptions are opposed, but the author of each is led by his conception to conclude that because of it the novel is the most important literary form in the modern world, and *for* the modern world. The first is from D. H. Lawrence, and it is, I believe, a unique conception:

> It is the way our sympathy flows and recoils that really determines our lives. And here lies the vast importance of the novel, properly handled. It can inform and lead into new places the flow of our sympathetic consciousness, and it can lead our sympathy away in recoil from things gone dead. Therefore, the novel, properly handled, can reveal the most secret places of life: for it is in the *passional* secret places of life, above all, that the tide of sensitive awareness needs to ebb and flow, cleansing and freshening.

> But the novel, like gossip, can also excite spurious sympathies and recoils, mechanical and deadening to the psyche. The novel can glorify the most corrupt feelings so long as they are *conventionally* "pure." Then the novel, like gossip, becomes at last vicious, and, like gossip, all the more vicious because it is always ostensibly on the side of the angels.

> [*Lady Chatterley's Lover*]

From *Sinclair Lewis: A Collection of Critical Essays*, edited by Mark Schorer. © 1962 by Mark Schorer.

Lawrence's conception implies a novel that will admit us directly into the
life-affirming activities of the integrated consciousness of his own ideal man;
a novel that, concerned with the formed individual consciousness, reforms
ours; a novel that is not about society or the social character but that is
ultimately indispensable to the health of both. We know whose fiction he
has in mind; we know, too, with what exasperation he achieved the first
term of his exalted ambition, the writing itself, and how impossible it is to
achieve the second, the therapy.

Our second quotation is a commonplace in the annals of American
naturalism, and we could find it, in substance, in any of a dozen writers.
Frank Norris will serve. I quote first from his essay, "The Responsibilities
of the Novelist," an attack on what he calls "lying novels," novels of sentiment
and romance.

> Today is the day of the novel. In no other day and by no other
> vehicle is contemporaneous life so adequately expressed; and the
> critics of the twenty-second century, reviewing our times, striving
> to reconstruct our civilization, will look not to the painters, not
> to the architects nor dramatists, but to the novelists to find our
> idiosyncrasy. . . . If the novel . . . is popular it is popular with
> a reason, a vital, inherent reason; that is to say, it is essential . . .
> it is an instrument, a tool, a weapon, a vehicle. Public opinion
> is made no one can say how, by infinitesimal accretions, by a
> multitude of minutest elements. Lying novels, surely in this day
> and age of indiscriminate reading, contribute to this more than
> all other influences of present-day activity . . . The People have
> a right to the Truth as they have a right to life, liberty and the
> pursuit of happiness. It is *not* right that they be exploited and
> deceived with false views of life, false characters, false sentiment,
> false morality, false history, false philosophy, false emotions, false
> heroism, false notions of self-sacrifice, false views of religion, of
> duty, of conduct and of manners.

And where do we find the truth-telling novel? In the novel with a "purpose,"
as it is discussed in the essay of that name.

> Every novel must do one of three things—it must (1) tell some-
> thing, (2) show something, or (3) prove something. Some novels
> do all three of these. . . . The third, and what we hold to be the
> best class, proves something, draws conclusions from a whole
> congeries of forces, social tendencies, race impulses, devotes itself

not to a study of men but of man. . . . Take this element from fiction, take from it the power and opportunity to prove that injustice, crime and inequality do exist, and what is left? Just the amusing novels, the novels that entertain . . . the modern novel . . . may be a flippant paper-covered thing of swords and cloaks, to be carried on a railway journey and to be thrown out the window when read, together with the sucked oranges and peanut shells. Or it may be a great force, that works together with the pulpit and the universities for the good of the people, fearlessly proving that power is abused, that the strong grind the faces of the weak, that an evil tree is still growing in the midst of the garden, that undoing follows hard upon righteousness, that the course of Empire is not yet finished, and that the races of men have yet to work out their destiny in those great and terrible movements that crush and grind and rend asunder the pillars of the houses of the nation.

It is within this somewhat crude conception of "the novel with a purpose" that we are accustomed to place the novels that brought Sinclair Lewis his fame. Lewis himself was not content to have his work thus located. In a heavily playful refutation of the charge that he was "a raging reformer, an embittered satirist, a realist dreary as cold gravy," he said:

I should have thought Brother Lewis was essentially a storyteller—just as naive, excited, unselfconscious as the Arab storytellers about the caravan fires seven hundred years ago, or as O. Henry in a hotel room on Twenty-third Street furiously turning out tales for dinner and red-ink money. In his stories Lewis does not happen to be amused only by the sea or by midnight encounters on the Avenue, but oftener by the adventure of the soul in religion and patriotism and social climbing. But they are essentially stories just the same.

The fact is that the novels we have in mind are not "essentially stories," that the "story" element is secondary and quite feebly managed; and that if they are not quite the "novel with a purpose" as Norris conceived it— motivated by an outraged sense of justice and executed with naturalistic fulness—their impulse is plainly the exposition of social folly. H. L. Mencken, some years after he had ceased to be a well-known literary critic, takes us to the center of Lewis's imaginative uniqueness when, in 1945, he congratulates him on a poor novel called *Cass Timberlane*, an exposure of the corruptions of marriage in the middle class:

I am not going to tell you that "Cass Timerblane" is comparable
to "Babbitt" or "Elmer Gantry" (all except the last 30,000 words,
which you wrote in a state of liquor), but it seems to me to be
the best thing you have done, and by long odds, since "Dodsworth." . . . In brief, a well-planned and well-executed book,
with a fine surface. . . . The country swarms with subjects for
your future researches. You did the vermin of the Coolidge era,
but those of the Roosevelt and post-Roosevelt eras are still open—
the rich radical, the bogus expert, the numskull newspaper pro-
prietor (or editor), the career-jobholder, the lady publicist, the
crooked (or, more usually, idiotic) labor leader, the press-agent,
and so on. This, I believe is your job, and you have been ne-
glecting it long enough. There are plenty of writers of love stories
and Freudian documents, though not many as good at it as you
are, but there is only one real anatomist of the American Kultur.
I think it stinks, but whether it stinks or not is immaterial. It
deserves to be done as you alone can do it.

The catalogue of social types is the significant item in this letter. Each
of these with its implied section of social life in the United States, could
have become a Lewis novel. Some already had. With Lewis, the subject,
the social section, always came first; systematic research sometimes conducted by research assistants and carrying Lewis himself into "the field" like
any cultural anthropologist, followed; the story came last, devised to carry
home and usually limping under the burden of data. If the result in some
ways filled the Norris prescription for a novel of the contemporary social
character, it was still by no means a naturalistic product; at the same time,
precisely what was "new" in it was what D. H. Lawrence called "dead,"
and he would have howled in outrage at the complacency with which Lewis
asserted that his stories described "the adventure of the soul in religion and
patriotism." For in the world of Sinclair Lewis there is no soul, and if a soul
were introduced into it, it would die on the instant.

The world of Sinclair Lewis rests upon two observations: the standardization of manners in a business culture, and the stultification of morals
under middle-class convention. All his critical observations are marshalled
in support of these propositions, and his portrait of the middle class rests
entirely upon them. The proliferation of detail within these observations
gives them an apparent breadth, and his easy familiarity with the manners—
in Robert Cantwell's catalogue—of "the small towns and square cities, the
real-estate developments and restricted residential areas, the small business

men, the country doctors, the religious fakers, the clubwomen, the county officeholders, the village atheists and single-taxers, the schoolteachers, librarians, the windbags of the lower income groups, the crazy professors and the maddened, hyperthyroid, high-pressure salesmen—the main types of middle-class and lower-middle-class provincial society, conspicuous now because he has identified them so thoroughly" ("Sinclair Lewis," in *After the Genteel Tradition*, ed. Malcolm Cowley)—all this gives his observations an apparent richness and variety; yet in fact it is all there in support of the extremely limited program. Similarly, his world is broken into many social sections—the small town, business ethics, medical science, evangelical religion, marriage, the career woman, professional philanthropy—and this is to name only those that come most immediately to mind; but every section rests, again, on one or both of the two primary principles. This is an extremely narrow and intellectually feeble perspective, but given the particular character of Lewis's achievement, its force paradoxically rests upon its narrowness.

For its narrowness projects a very sharply defined image. "Life dehumanized by indifference or enmity to all human values—that is the keynote of both Gopher Prairie and Zenith," wrote T. K. Whipple nearly thirty years ago in what remains one of the very few critical essays on Lewis, and one to which my own essay is much indebted:

> Nowhere does this animosity show itself more plainly than in hostility to truth and art. The creed of both towns is the philosophy of boosting, a hollow optimism and false cheeriness which leads directly to hypocrisy, as in making believe that business knavery is social service. Toward ideas likely to break this bubble of pretense the people are bitterly opposed; toward new ideas they are lazily contemptuous; toward other ideas they are apathetic . . . intellectually both are cities of the dead, and in both, the dead are resolved that no one shall live.

Dead in the senses as they are in intellect and the affections, these people are horrible ciphers, empty of personality or individual consciousness, rigidly controlled by set social responses; and yet, being dead, together they do not form a society in any real sense, but only a group, a group which at once controls them and protects them from the horrors of their own emptiness. Their group activities, whether as families, as clubs, as friends, are travesties of that human interchange that makes for meaningful social activities: conversation is buffoonery, affection is noise, gaiety is pretense, business is brutal rush, religion is blasphemy. The end result is vacant social types in

a nonsocial world. Quite brilliantly T. K. Whipple made and Maxwell
Geismar developed the observation that *Babbitt* is set in Hell: "it is almost
a perfectly conceived poetic vision of a perfectly . . . standardized hinterland"
(*The Last of the Provincials: The American Novel, 1915–1925*).

Poetic, that is to say, in the sense that it *is* visionary, *not* documentary,
so that nothing is either a lie or the truth. These are categories that have no
relevance. Collecting his massive accumulations of social data with the nat-
uralist's compulsiveness, Lewis creates a visual world and a world of manners
that appear to be absolutely solid, absolutely concrete; but all that accumulation of data has from the outset been made to submit so severely to the
selective strictures of two highly limited and limiting observations that what
emerges in fact is an image and a criticism of middle-class society and not
in the least a representation of it. A fragment blown into the proportions of
the whole, it is a fantastic world dominated by monstrous parodies of human
nature. Elmer Gantry, in his hypocrisy and self-deception, his brutal cruelty
and fearful faith, his shallow optimism and wretched betrayals, his almost
automatic identification of salvation and economic success, his loathing of
all thought, his hatred of all human difference, his incapacity for any feelings
but lust and fear and self-interest: in all this he carries to its extreme Sinclair
Lewis's conception of the middle-class character. Both the paradox and the
secret of such a creation lie in the fact that, except for the power of observation, the sensibility of the creator has few resources beyond those of the
thing created, that Lewis's own intellectual and moral framework, and the
framework of feeling, is extremely narrow, hardly wider than the material
it contains. And the power of the creation, I would insist, lies in these
limitations.

The limitations are so apparent that we need do little more than name
them. As his conception of middle-class society is fragmentary, so his sense
of history is vestigial. The characteristic widening of his shutter over social
space does not qualify or alter the narrow social conception:

> Eight thousand radio-owners listening to Elmer Gantry—A boot-
> legger in his flat, coat off, exposing his pink silk shirt, his feet
> up on the table. . . . The house of a small-town doctor, with the
> neighbors come in to listen—the drugstore man, his fat wife, the
> bearded superintendent of schools. . . . Mrs. Sherman Reeves of
> Royal Ridge, wife of one of the richest young men in Zenith,
> listening in a black-and-gold dressing-gown, while she smoked a
> cigarette. . . . The captain of a schooner, out on Lake Michigan,
> hundreds of miles away, listening in his cabin. . . . The wife of

a farmer in an Indiana valley, listening while her husband read the Sears-Roebuck catalogue and sniffed. . . . A retired railway conductor, very feeble, very religious. . . . A Catholic priest, in a hospital, chuckling a little. . . . A spinster schoolteacher, mad with loneliness, worshiping Dr. Gantry's virile voice. . . . Forty people gathered in a country church too poor to have a pastor. . . . A stock actor in his dressing-room, fagged with an all-night rehearsal.

All of them listening to the Rev. Dr. Elmer Gantry as he shouted.

Similarly, the characteristic extensions into time do not enrich the sense of history but merely provide broadly ironic contrasts that are analogically meaningless, both in the drama and in the intellectual framework:

So Elmer came, though tardily, to the Great Idea which was to revolutionize his life and bring him eternal and splendid fame.

That shabby Corsican artillery lieutenant and author, Bonaparte, first conceiving that he might be the ruler of Europe— Darwin seeing dimly the scheme of evolution —Paolo realizing that all of life was nothing but an irradiation of Francesca— Newton pondering on the falling apple—Paul of Tarsus comprehending that a certain small Jewish sect might be the new religion of the doubting Greeks and Romans—Keats beginning to write "The Eve of St. Agnes"—none of these men, transformed by a Great Idea from mediocrity to genius, was more remarkable than Elmer Gantry of Paris, Kansas, when he beheld the purpose for which the heavenly powers had been training him.

The characters of this world are aware of no tradition within which their lives are located; behind them lies no history except for the faintly heroic figure of a pioneer whose sacrifice their lives have made meaningless. And if the seat of this deficiency is in the imagination of the author, its result is the captive blankness of their existence, which is a large element in the egregious parody.

From an early if not very forcibly held socialist position, Sinclair Lewis, in his best novels, swung round to the antidemocratic views of H. L. Mencken; yet paradoxically, he had no values of his own (not even Mencken's vague Nietzscheanism) except those of the middle-class that both were lampooning. The ambition to find in the East what is not available in the Midwest is always exposed as false; and when "the East" is pushed on to mean Europe, the same evaluation is made. The Midwest is shown as hopelessly narrow, yet somehow it is shown finally as the only sensible place to choose. Aristocrats are suspect if not phony; workmen tend to become shiftless mongrels; intellectuals and artists are irresponsible bohemians. The picture of middle-class provincialism is framed by a middle-class provincial view. "Russian Jews in London clothes," Lewis writes in *Dodsworth*, "going to Italian restaurants with Greek waiters and African music." And again, if the deficiency in a sense of tradition and of history is the author's own, it contributes to the force of his image, for it permits his characters no escape. Always excepting the figures of Doctors Gottlieb and Arrowsmith, with their dedication to pure science, the dissident figures in Lewis's novels, the critics of this society, are permitted no realizable values toward which they or that society may aspire.

The febblest characters in *Main Street*, and those most quickly routed, are the discontented. Carol Kennicott's vaporous values are the equivalent of that deeply sentimental strain in the author that led him as a young man to write in imitation of the early Tennyson and, as a man of over fifty, to say that "he, who has been labeled a 'satirist' and a 'realist,' is actually a romantic medievalist of the most incurable sort." Thus Carol:

> a volume of Yeats on her knees. . . . Instantly she was released
> from the homely comfort of a prairie town. She was in the world
> of lonely things—the flutter of twilight linnets, the aching call
> of gulls along a shore to which the netted foam crept out of
> darkness, the island of Aengus and the elder gods and the eternal
> glories that never were, tall kings and women girdled with crusted
> gold, the woeful incessant chanting.

Thus the Babbitt who momentarily challenges Zenith does not so much present us with a scale of humane values that we can oppose to the inhumanity of the environment, as he presents us with all the insecurity on which Babbittry, or the environment, rests. The fact that there is never any real opposition of substantial values to "convention," or false values (as there is never any truly individual character to resist the social types), is what makes Lewis's world so blank and limits so drastically his social realism. In *Elmer Gantry* we do not have even these fitful glimmerings in the realm of reverie. This is a world of total death, of social monsters without shadow. It is, in my view and on rereading, the purest Lewis.

The publication of *Elmer Gantry* early in 1927 was not so much a literary event as it was a public scandal, and from the beginning, therefore, excitement took the place of criticism. Preceded by the well-publicized "Strike me dead" episode, it called forth remarks like this from William Allen White:

"Sinclair Lewis stood in the pulpit of a Kansas City church last spring and defied God to strike him dead. So far as Sinclair Lewis, the artist, is concerned in the book 'Elmer Gantry,' God took him at his word." Municipal bans extended from Kansas City to Camden; from Boston to Glasgow. Its initial printing of 140,000 copies was probably the largest to that date of any book in history, and the whole emphasis of the promotion campaign was on the *size* of the enterprise: the book was advertised on billboards; a publicity release from the publishers was headed "What it Means to Manufacture the First Edition of *Elmer Gantry*," and provided statistics on amounts of paper, thread, glue, board, cloth, and ink, both black and orange—black for the text, orange for the cover. (But then, as Lewis tells us in the novel, "Elmer was ever a lover of quantity.") In April of 1927, in a resolution supporting the Anti-Saloon League of New York State, the Rev. Dr. Otho F. Bartholow declared at the annual session of the New York East Conference, "The Methodist Church is cordially hated, not only by the class represented by Mr. Sinclair Lewis and the rum organizations, but also by every evil organization of every kind whatsoever," while, two weeks later, the graduating class of New York University voted Sinclair Lewis its favorite author. A news item in an Ohio newspaper ran as follows:

> Trouble in the home of Leo Roberts, general manager of the Roberts Coal and Supply Company, began when his wife brought home a copy of "Elmer Gantry" and he burned it as undesirable reading matter, according to Mrs. Roberts at a hearing Wednesday before Judge Bostwick, of Probate Court, when Roberts was ordered to a private sanitarium for a short rest, after his wife, Mrs. Margaret Roberts, 1671 Franklin Park South, charged him with lunacy.

Literary appraisal seems to have been a quite secondary matter. Yet, if only because the images that Lewis projected came to play such a powerful role in the imagination both of America and of Europe, it is worth our time to analyze the method or lack of method that established them. Leslie Fiedler recently wrote as follows:

> no one has succeeded since the age of Sinclair Lewis and Sherwood Anderson in seeing an actual American small town or a living member of the Kiwanis club. The gross pathos of Anderson or the journalistic thinness of Lewis is beside the point; for all of us, the real facts of experience have been replaced by Winesburg, Ohio and by Babbitt; myth or platitude, we have invented nothing to replace them. ["The Ant on the Grasshopper," *Partisan Review* (Summer, 1955)]

How, then, did *he* invent them? What props up and holds in place that terrifying buffoon, Elmer Gantry—that "gladiator laughing at the comic distortion of his wounded opponent," as he sees himself; that "barytone solo turned into portly flesh," as Lewis shows him to us?

The primary fact in Lewis's method is the absence of conflict between genuine orders of value, and in *Elmer Gantry* this fact emerges most starkly.

In *Elmer Gantry*, any drama exists in the immediate victory of the worst over the weakest (who are the best), or in the struggle of the bad to survive among the worst: all is corrupt. In this extraordinarily full account of every form of religious decay, nothing is missing except all religion and all humanity. As there are no impediments to Elmer's barbarous rise from country boob to influential preacher, so there are no qualifications of the image of barbarity. On the very fringes of the narrative, among his scores of characters, Lewis permits a few shadowy figures of good to appear—Bruno Zechlin and Jim Lefferts, the amiable skeptics who are routed before they are permitted to enter the action; Andrew Pengilly, a humane preacher who asks the most striking question in the novel ("Mr. Gantry, why don't you believe in God?") but who himself no more enters the story than his question enters the intellectual context; and finally, Frank Shallard, who does come and go in the story, an honest human being, but one so weak that he presents no challenge to Elmer, serves only to illustrate the ruthlessness of Elmer's power.

In the novel, values can be realized only in action, and the action of *Elmer Gantry* is an entirely one-way affair. This is the inevitable consequence in structure of Lewis's method. Like most of Lewis's novels, *Elmer Gantry* is a loosely episodic chronicle, which suggests at once that there will be no sustained pressure of plot, no primary conflict about which all the action is organized and in which value will achieve a complex definition or in which that dramatization of at least two orders of value that conflict implies will be brought about. The chronicle breaks down into three large parts, each pretty nearly independent of the others. In each event Elmer's progress is colored and in two of them threatened by his relation with a woman, but from each Elmer emerges triumphant. The first part takes us through his Baptist education, his ordination, his first pulpit, and his escape from Lulu; the second takes us through his career as an evangelist with the fantastic Sharon Falconer; the third takes us through his experience of New Thought and his rise in Methodism, together with the decline of his marriage to Cleo and his escape from Hettie, who threatens to bring him to public ruin but who is herself routed as, in the final sentence, Elmer promises that "We shall yet make these United States a moral nation."

It should not be supposed that the frank prominence in *Elmer Gantry* of sexual appetite—a rare enough element in a Lewis novel—or the fact that it several times seems to threaten Elmer's otherwise unimpeded success, in any way provides the kind of dramatized counterpoint on the absence of which we are remarking, or that it in any way serves to introduce an element of human tenderness that qualifies Elmer's brutal nakedness. On the contrary, it is an integral part of his inhumanity and an integral part of the inhumanity of the religious environment within which he exists. Indeed, of all the forms of relationship that the novel presents, the sexual relation is most undilutedly brutish, and it is perhaps the chief element in that animus of revulsion that motivates the creation of this cloacal world and upon which I shall presently comment. Finally, its identification with the quality of Elmer's religous activity is made explicit in the climactically phantasmagoric scene in which Sharon capitulates to Elmer before an altar where she associates herself, in a ritual invocation, with all goddesses of fertility.

"It is the hour! Blessed Virgin, Mother Hera, Mother Frigga, Mother Ishtar, Mother Isis, dread Mother Astarte of the weaving arms, it is thy priestess, it is she who after the blind centuries and the groping years shall make it known to the world that ye are one, and that in me are ye all revealed, and that in this revelation shall come peace and wisdom universal, the secret of the spheres and the pit of understanding. Ye who have leaned over me and on my lips pressed your immortal fingers, take this my brother to your bosoms, open his eyes, release his pinioned spirit, make him as the gods, that with me he may carry the revelation for which a thousand thousand grievous years the world has panted.

"Ye veiled ones and ye bright ones—from caves forgotten, the peaks of the future, the clanging today—join in me, lift up, receive him, dread nameless ones; yea, lift us then, mystery on mystery, sphere above sphere, dominion on dominion, to the very throne!

"O mystical rose, O lily most admirable, O wondrous union; O St. Anna, Mother Immaculate, Demeter, Mother Beneficient, Lakshmi, Mother Most Shining; behold, I am his and he is yours and ye are mine!"

The extravagant absurdity of this scene is underlined by the absence in it of any candid recognition of human need or of human fulfillment. The travesty that it makes of both the sexual and the religous experience is of course to be associated with the temper of orgiastic evangelism with which the book is full. Dramatically, however, it must be associated with such an earlier scene, as homely as this one is horrendous, in which a deaf old retired preacher and his wife are going to bed after fifty years of marriage and the whole of that experience of fifty years is equated with an "old hoss."

They were nodding on either side of a radiator unheated for months.

"All right, Emmy," piped the ancient.

"Say, Papa—Tell me: I've been thinking: If you were just a young man today would you go into the ministry?"

"Course I would! What an idea! Most glorious vocation young man could have. Idea! G'night, Emmy!"

But as his ancient wife sighingly removed her corsets, she complained, "Don't know as you would or not—if *I* was married to you—which ain't any too certain, a second time—and if I had anything to say about it!"

"Which *is* certain! Don't be foolish. Course I would."

"I don't know. Fifty years I had of it, and I never did get so I wa'n't just mad clear through when the ladies of the church came poking around, criticizing me for every little tidy I put on the chairs, and talking something terrible if I had a bonnet or a shawl that was the least mite tasty. ''Twant suitable for a minister's wife.' Drat 'em! And I always did like a bonnet with some nice bright colors. Oh, I've done a right smart of thinking about it. You always were a powerful preacher, but's I've told you—"

"You have!"

"—I never could make out how, if when you were in the pulpit you really knew so much about all these high and mighty and mysterious things, how it was when you got home you never knew enough, and you never could learn enough, to find the hammer or make a nice piece of cornbread or add up a column of figures twice alike or find Oberammergau on the map of Austria!"

"Germany, woman! I'm sleepy!"

"And all these years of having to pretend to be so good when we were just common folks all the time! Ain't you glad you can just be simple folks now?"

"Maybe it is restful. But that's not saying I wouldn't do it over again." The old man ruminated a long while. "I think I would. Anyway, no use discouraging these young people from entering the ministry. Somebody got to preach the gospel truth, ain't they?"

"I suppose so. Oh, dear. Fifty years since I married a preacher! And if I could still only be sure about the virgin birth! Now don't you go explaining! Laws, the number of times you've explained! I know it's true—it's in the Bible. If I could only *believe* it! But—

"I would of liked to had you try your hand at politics. If I could of been, just once, to a senator's house, to a banquet or something, just once, in a nice bright red dress with gold slippers, I'd of been willing to go back to alpaca and scrubbing floors and listening to you rehearsing your sermons, out in the stable, to that old mare we had for so many years—oh, laws, how long is it she's been dead now? Must be—yes, it's twenty-seven years—

"Why is it that it's only in religion that the things you got to believe are agin all experience? Now drat it, don't you go and quote that 'I believe because it *is* impossible' thing at me again! Believe because it's impossible! Huh! Just like a minister!

"Oh, dear, I hope I don't live long enough to lose my faith. Seems like the older I get, the less I'm excited over all these preachers that talk about hell only they never saw it.

"Twenty-seven years! And we had that old hoss so long before that. My how she could kick—Busted that buggy—"

They were both asleep.

The two scenes, the extravagantly repulsive and the devastatingly barren, supplement one another; they represent the extremes of the nightmare image of a world that, totally empty of human value, monstrously, and without relief, parodies the reality.

If the narrative method of loose chronicle, without sustained dramatic conflict, is the primary means to this end, certain orders of technical detail contribute no less and seem entirely consistent with the imagination that is working through the narrative method. It has been complained, for example, that there is a coarsening of Lewis's style in this novel, and that his view of the hinterland threatens to fall into a kind of crackerbarrel stereotype. Both charges are true, but it can be argued that both qualities make possible the kind of effect we are trying to describe. *Elmer Gantry* is the noisiest novel in American literature, the most *braying, guffawing, belching* novel that we have, and it is its prose that sets this uproar going; if we are to have a novel filled with jackasses and jackals, let them, by all means, bray and guffaw. On the same grounds, I would defend the "By crackee, by jiminy" crudities of the physical environment within which this noise goes on, this imbecilic articulateness, only pointing out in addition that Lewis's old ability to invoke a concrete world—the smell of Pullman car dust, the food at a church picnic, the contents of the library of a small Methodist bishop—is still sufficiently in force to cram full the outlines of his stereotypes. One can go further. At each of his three climaxes, Lewis abdicates such sense of the dramatic scene as he may have had and retreats into melodrama: once to an inversion of the farmer's daughter situation, once to a catastrophic fire, finally to a cops-and-robbers treatment of some petty criminals who have attempted to play the badger game on old Elmer. In each situation, through bad timing, through a refusal to develop even a suggestion of suspense, any potential human elements in the situation are sacrificed to the melodramatic stereotype. And yet, out of this very weakness, cumulatively, arises again the whole impression of bare brutality which is, after all, the essential social observation. As the drama is only half realized, so the social observation is only half true, but in its partiality resides such force of which it is capable.

Most novels operate through a conflict, dramatized in a plot, of social and individual interest, and the more sustained the pressures of the plot, the more likely is the individual to be forced into a position of new self-awareness, which prominently contains an awareness of his relation to his society. A certain dynamic interchange has been at work, and the result is that the historical forces which contain the individual's experience have been personalized in his awareness. What is most characteristic of the novels of Sinclair Lewis, and above all of *Elmer Gantry*, is the fact that there are no such dynamics of social action, that we are presented with a static unpersonalized image—and that *there* lies its horror.

Elmer Gantry has perhaps one brief moment of honesty. He has come to Sharon's fantastic home, he is looking out upon the river, he fancies himself in love:

> "Shen-an-doah!" he crooned.
> Suddenly he was kneeling at the window, and for the first time since he had forsaken Jim Lefferts and football and joyous ribaldry, his soul was free of all the wickedness which had daubed it—oratorical ambitions, emotional orgasm, dead sayings of dull seers, dogmas, and piety. The golden winding river drew him, the sky uplifted him, and with outflung arms he prayed for deliverance from prayer.

"I've found her. Sharon. Oh, I'm not going on with this evangelistic bunk. Trapping idiots into holy monkey-shines! No, by
God, I'll be honest! I'll tuck her under my arm and go out and
fight. Business. Put it over. Build something big. And laugh, not
snivel and shake hands with church-members! I'll do it!"

Then and there his rebellion against himself ends, and after that he knows
nothing of self-recognition. This is about as close to it as he can come:

"I'll have a good time with those folks," he reflected, in the
luxury of a taxicab. "Only, better be careful with old Rigg. He's
a shrewd bird, and he's onto me. . . . Now what do you mean?"
indignantly. "What do you mean by 'onto me'? There's nothing
to be onto! I refused a drink and a cigar, didn't I? I never cuss
except when I lose my temper, do I? I'm leading an absolutely
Christian life. And I'm bringing a whale of a lot more souls into
churches than any of these pussy-footing tin saints that're afraid
to laugh and jolly people. 'Onto me' nothing!"

A character so open to self-deception is not in a position to estimate the
forces that have made him so: to him, society is given, accepted, used. Elmer
Gantry was raised in an important if stultifying American tradition: the
Protestantism of the hinterland; and Sinclair Lewis gives us a complete and
devastating account of it that extends over four pages and from which I now
draw fragments, reluctantly omitting Lewis's substantiating body of detail:

The church and Sunday School at Elmer's village . . . had nur-
tured in him a fear of religious machinery which he could never
lose. . . . That small pasty-white Baptist church had been the
center of all his emotions, aside from hell-raising, hunger, sleep-
iness, and love. And even these emotions were represented in the
House of the Lord . . . the arts and the sentiments and the sen-
timentalities—they were for Elmer perpetually associated only
with the church . . . all the music which the boy Elmer had ever
heard was in church . . . it provided all his painting and sculp-
ture. . . . From the church came all his profounder philosophy
. . . literary inspiration . . . here too the church had guided him.
In Bible stories, in the words of the great hymns, in the anecdotes
which the various preachers quoted, he had his only knowledge
of literature. . . . The church, the Sunday School, the evangelistic orgy, choir-practise, raising the mortgage, the delights of
funerals, the snickers in back pews or in the other room at wed-

dings—they were . . . a mold of manners to Elmer. . . . Sunday
School text cards . . . they gave him a taste for gaudy robes, for
marble columns and the purple-broidered palaces of kings, which
was later to be of value in quickly habituating himself to the more
decorative homes of vice. . . . And always the three chairs that
stood behind the pulpit, the intimidating stiff chairs of yellow
plush and carved oak borders, which, he was uneasily sure, were
waiting for the Father, the Son, and the Holy Ghost.

He had, in fact, got everything from the church and Sunday
School, except, perhaps, any longing whatever for decency and
kindness and reason.

And having neither decency nor kindness nor reason (as the novel contains
no animated examples of these humane virtues), Elmer is necessarily unaware
of the history in which he is involved.

That history, perhaps no larger than it is beautiful in our tradition, is
nevertheless considerable, and Sinclair Lewis was aware of it even if, because
he had no alternatives, he could not let his characters become so. (The
tradition survives, of course: a Madison Avenue patina, extending from
Washington, D.C., to Whittier, California, does not alter the motives of
cynically opportunistic politicians; it merely moves boorish Elmer into gray
flannel and the seat of power). The whole brutally accurate conception of
R. H. Tawney, which coupled business success and salvation, and then, in
popular culture, began to pay dividends on the "saved" soul; the obvious
connection between the Puritan repressions (I use Lewis's terms, not mine)
and the orgiastic outbursts of middle-border evangelism; the Gospel of Service (made in Zenith) becoming the equivalent of the Gospels—all this is in
the author's mind as he creates his characters, but the very nature of his
creation prohibits it from in any way sharing his knowledge. The result is
that the Lewis character cannot separate itself from the Lewis society; and
this, in the dynamics of fiction, means that the Lewis character *has* no character apart from the society in which it is embedded, and that therefore the
Lewis society is not a society at all, but a machine. And this is the moral,
for criticism as for life today, of Lewis's novels, and expecially of this one.

"All vital truth," said D. H. Lawrence, "contains the memory of all
that for which it is not true." And Frank Norris, that infinitely simpler man,
said, "You must be something more than a novelist if you can, something
more than just a writer. There must be that nameless sixth sense or sensibility
. . . the thing that does not enter into the work, but that is back of it." Here
these two unlikely companions become companionable: both are asking for

a certain reverberating largeness behind any concretely conceived situation if that situation is to echo back into the great caverns of the human condition. This quality, I think, even a partisan could not claim that Sinclair Lewis had. Almost justly, Robert Cantwell described him as one "who thought of his writing, not in terms of its momentary inspirations and the . . . pressure of living that played through him and upon him, but in terms of the accomplishment of a foreknown task"; and almost plausibly, Maxwell Geismar wrote that "Just as there is really no sense of vice in Lewis's literary world, there is no true sense of virtue. Just as there is practically no sense of human love in the whole range of Lewis's psychological values, and no sense of real hatred—there is no genuine sense of human freedom." Most of this indictment one may allow, but if we are speaking specifically of *Elmer Gantry*, we would wish to insist on two of the items that these descriptions deny him: "the pressure of living that played through him and upon him," and the "hatred."

Elmer Gantry is a work of almost pure revulsion. It seems to shudder and to shake with loathing of that which it describes. The very fact that the novelist must create the image of the thing he loathes, in order to express his loathing, points to the peculiar imaginative animus that motivates this novel. We can speculate about its sources: Lewis's own early evangelistic impulse, his dedication to the missionary field now turning in upon itself; the lonely, goofy boy at Oberlin, himself pushing the handles of a handcar (as Elmer Gantry does) to get to a rural Sunday School where, without conspicuous success, he doled out Bible stories; the poor fool of the hinterland at New Haven, who had never been given more by the hinterland than the dubious gift of deriding it, and therefore of having to love it. Perhaps such speculations are not much to the point. The point is only that in no novel does Sinclair Lewis more clearly announce his loathing of the social environment with which he is concerned, and in no novel does he make it more mandatory that we remain within the terrifying limits of that environment.

Sinclair Lewis is not unlike Elmer Gantry. The vicious circle in this picture exists, of course, in the fact that Elmer remakes society in precisely the terms that society has already made him. No one can break out; everyone, including the novelist, spins more madly in the mechanical orbit.

The novelist trapped in his own hallucination of the world as a trap: this seems to be the final observation that we can make. But it is not quite final. Finally, we are left with the hallucination of the novels themselves, with their monstrous images of what we both are and are not, their nearly fabulous counter-icons in our culture. They stand somewhere between the two conceptions of the novel with which we began: they tell us too much

of why we are dead and not enough of how we can live to satisfy the
prescription either of Lawrence or of Norris, deprived as they are of all that
psychic affirmation that would meet the demands of the first, and of most
of that social realism that would meet those of the second. But they have—
for this very reason—their *own* quality. If that quality is of the half-truth,
and the half-truth has moved back into our way of estimating our society,
the judgment falls on us, on our own failure of observation and imagination.
If we accept the half-truth for the fact, then the novel is indeed the most
important literary instrument in and for our world; and we can only lament
the inability, not of our novelists to provide the stimulus, but of ourselves
to repel it, of our failure, in the sympathetic consciousness, to recoil from
it. *Elmer Gantry* reminds us that we continue to embrace as fervently as we
deny this horror that at least in part we are.

CHARLES E. ROSENBERG

Martin Arrowsmith: The Scientist as Hero

With the manuscript of *Babbitt* almost complete in the fall of 1921, Sinclair Lewis already planned his next novel. "Perhaps," he wrote Alfred Harcourt, his friend and publisher, it would not be satiric at all, "rebellious as ever, . . . but the central character *heroic*." His next novel was *Arrowsmith*. Its heroic protagonist is a research scientist, the first of consequence in American fiction. To Sinclair Lewis he was far more than that.

Martin Arrowsmith is a new kind of hero, one appropriate to twentieth-century America. Journalists and historians tirelessly inform us that the 1920s were years of intense and aggressive materialism. Yet Arrowsmith is quite obviously a hero not of deeds, but of the spirit. His scientific calling is not a concession to material values, but a means of overcoming them. In the austere world of pure science and in the example of Max Gottlieb, Arrowsmith finds a system of values which guide and sanction his stumbling quest for personal integrity. It is this quest which provides the novel's moral structure. Martin Arrowsmith's professional career is the record of his deepening understanding and acceptance of these scientific values and of their role in assuring Arrowsmith's ultimate triumph in his struggles with a succession of increasingly plausible material temptations.

Other centuries have accepted patterns into which such moral achievement could be projected—the martyr, the pilgrim, the evangelist and, in more recent generations, the creative artist. None of these seemed particularly relevant to Sinclair Lewis in 1922. He had emphatically rejected the

From *American Quarterly* 15, no. 3 (Fall 1963). © 1963 by the Trustees of the University of Pennsylvania.

forms of traditional religion, despite the appeal which they had held for him as a lonely adolescent. Religion had become just another marketable commodity; its purveyors could not easily be pictured as heroic. Nor was the sensitive artist a potential hero; Lewis knew too many and knew them too well. Yet Sinclair Lewis was very much a novelist of society, very much bound to the particular. His hero had to have a vocation. The problem was to find one in which dignity and integrity could be maintained in a world of small compromise and petty accommodation.

Yet America did have a heritage of dignity and individualism, Lewis believed. It lay in the pioneering spirit of the men and women who had settled the nation's West. Their heroic qualities had created America, yet theirs were the very characteristics which seemed to be disappearing most rapidly in a twentieth-century America, settled and implacably confining. *Arrowsmith* begins with an almost crudely pointed vignette: Martin Arrowsmith's great-grandmother, aged fourteen, is seated at the reins of a wagon. Her father, lying racked with fever in the wagon's bed, begs her to turn aside and ask shelter at her uncle's. But she will be obligated to no one and turns the wagon west. "They's a whole lot of new things I aim to be seeing," she exclaims. On the opening page of *Main Street*, Lewis describes another restless young girl. Carol Milford, like Arrowsmith, is the descendent of pioneers. Though the days of their exploits are "deader than Camelot," the spirit of her daring ancestors survives to animate this rebellious girl. In the future Mrs. Kennicott, however, the divine discontent which helped people a continent becomes an unfocused and almost pathetic dissatisfaction with the commonplace world of Gopher Prairie. Arrowsmith is gifted with the same vigor and curiosity—but is able to attain through it the heroic stature denied Carol. In the life of the pure scientist he discovers a vocation in which his spiritual endowments find meaningful and constructive expression.

During the early part of 1922, the *Century Magazine* published a series of anonymous articles attacking the pretensions of American medicine. The articles were entitled "Our Medicine Men," and written by Paul de Kruif, a junior staff member at the Rockefeller Institute. By the end of 1922 he was unemployed.

In the summer of 1922, Sinclair Lewis still sought a suitable protagonist for his heroic novel. He had begun his customarily detailed research for a novel of the American labor movement, its hero to be a Christlike leader modeled after Eugene Debs. But the novel did not seem to coalesce. On a hot August day in Chicago, Morris Fishbein, associate editor of the *Journal of the American Medical Association*, introduced Lewis to the young bacteriologist from the Rockefeller Institute. *Arrowsmith* was the result of this meeting. No one but Sinclair Lewis could have written quite such a novel, yet insofar as *Arrowsmith* is a comment on the world of American medicine and biological research, insofar as it makes use of scientific values and preoccupations, it reflects clearly the attitudes of Paul de Kruif.

De Kruif provided Lewis with the *vitae* for his principal characters, with the details of laboratory procedure and with a plausible scientific setting for Arrowsmith's exploits. Even more important, Lewis believed, was his contribution of the scientist's "philosophy." De Kruif entertained few doubts concerning the nature of the scientific endeavor or of the intellectual and personal integrity it demanded. He was equally certain that most American research was slipshod and careless, simply cluttering the journals and indices. De Kruif's influence can be documented not only in Sinclair Lewis's own words, but in the youthful bacteriologist's published writings. Before the appearance of *Arrowsmith* in March of 1925, he had written, in addition to the articles in the *Century*, an essay on Jacques Loeb which appeared in *Harper's* and the section on medicine, also anonymous, in Harold Stearns's *Civilization in the United States*. His discussion of Loeb, both in *Harper's* and in Stearns's *Civilization*, is particularly significant, for it is Jacques Loeb's values which are those professed by Max Gottlieb. De Kruif's "philosophy" is not a philosophy at all, but the recent convert's overenthusiastic reflection of a philosophy—of Loeb's biological mechanism.

Loeb's methodological scruples, even his style of life, had, moreover, a particular significance for American medicine in the early 1920s. He lived and expressed the gospel of pure science. In at least a limited sense, *Arrowsmith* is an incident in the birth of a new scientific medicine. De Kruif's hostility toward the medical profession is an extreme, though not unrepresentative, instance of the laboratory scientist's hostility toward the clinician. Such attitudes, formed in the uneasy coexistence between laboratory and clinical medicine, shaped many of the particular incidents and emphases in *Arrowsmith*.

Martin Arrowsmith's professional biography is a record not only of the progress of a confused and easily misled young man toward emotional and intellectual fulfillment; it is the recapitulation in one man's life of the development of medicine in the United States. Each stage of Arrowsmith's career corresponds to a particular stage in the evolution of American medicine. Doc Vickerson's practice—and Martin's own practice in Wheatsylvania—dramatizes, for example, the trials and rewards of what De Kruif called "the splendid old type of general practitioner." Both he and Lewis were sympathetic to this aspect of American medicine. It seemed informal, individual, at moments even heroic; at least it was free of that mixture of ersatz science and sordid commercialism which De Kruif regarded as having corrupted contemporary medical practice.

At Winnemac University, both teachers and classmates of young Arrowsmith exemplify particular types and trends in medicine's coming-of-age. Dean Silva, for example, the pious disciple of Osler and Laennec, represents the understanding and craftsmanship to be found in clinical medicine. Professor Robertshaw, the self-exiled Brahmin physiologist, who always spoke—with elaborate casualness—of his student days in Leipzig with Carl Ludwig, illustrates the transference of German laboratory medicine to the United States—and with his "fussy little . . . maiden-aunt experiments" proves that the progress of science demands the spirit and not simply the techniques of German science. Roscoe Geake, the professor of otolaryngology and future minion of the New Idea Instrument and Furniture Company, is a representative of the most sordid and ignoble aspects of clinical medicine, his specialism simply a device for the multiplication of fees.

Unlike most of his fellow medical students, Arrowsmith is the graduate of a four-year liberal arts curriculum. He is confident in his abilities as he enters medical school and looks forward to increasing his scientific knowledge. But, except for the inspiring example of Max Gottlieb, he is to be sadly disappointed. Arrowsmith's disillusionment is identical with that experienced by a hypothetical college graduate whose medical career was depected by Paul de Kruif in the *Century*. He

> enters his first medical course with confidence, aware of his superiority over the majority of his fellows. It is easy, then, to imagine his dismay when he discovers that he knows far more of physics and chemistry than many of his medical instructors, and finds himself surrounded by glib-memoried, poorly-prepared ignoramuses who shine by reason of their parrot-like ability to reel off an enormous number of facts crammed out of text-books.

After a short residency at a metropolitan hospital, an experience which at first stimulates then bores him, Arrowsmith begins practice in Wheatsylvania, North Dakota. But a newly inspired enthusiasm for public-health work earns him only the scorn of the small farming community. Fortunately, he is able to leave. Through the agency of Max Gottlieb and Gustav Sondelius, he obtains a position with the health department of a small Iowa city. In Nautilus, Arrowsmith's zeal quickly fades before the boosterism of his chief, the improbable Almus Pickerbaugh. Public-health programs, Martin discovers, are to be prosecuted in newspaper columns and on the lecture platform, not in the laboratory. De Kruif had, before meeting Lewis, re-corded his intense dislike for such "shouters for public health," for these "dubious Messiahs who combine the zealous fanaticism of the missionary with the Jesuitical cynicism of the politician." Boards of health, he argued, should be administered by engineers, statisticians and bacteriologists—not by half-educated physicians.

Driven finally from his post in Nautilus, Arrowsmith is forced to accept a position with that "most competent, most clean and brisk and visionless medical factory, the Rouncefield Clinic." In the early years of the 1920s, the clinic seemed to all observers the most advanced form of medical practice. And De Kruif, like many other laboratory men, had already demonstrated his distaste for these gilded repair shops. Research, Arrowsmith soon learns, is regarded simply as a means of securing free advertising for the clinic. After a year of bondage at the Rouncefield Clinic, Arrowsmith's first paper is published in the *Journal of Infectious Diseases* and he is offered a research position at the McGurk Institute (of course, Lewis's conception of the Rocke-feller Institute). At first Arrowsmith feels that he has reached a kind of scientific Elysium. He has a well-equipped laboratory, competent assistants, the company of his revered Max Gottlieb. Yet this too proves less than idyllic. Its demand for social graces, for premature publication, in short, its cultivation of success leads Arrowsmith toward his final and most important decision. He resigns from the Institute and joins his friend, the irreverent chemist Terry Wickett, who had already fled the compromising security of McGurk, at a wooded Vermont lake. Here, with a few like-minded inves-tigators, they plan to conduct years of uninterrupted research. Thus the novel ends; Arrowsmith has conquered the final and most plausible obstacle in his quest for personal integrity—he has renounced success itself. Or at least success by the ordinary standards of American life. Like Max Gottlieb Martin Arrowsmith is destined for fame, but in a world whose judgments are eternal, international and ultimately untouched by material considerations.

One of the tentative titles for *Arrowsmith* was *The Shadow of Max Gottlieb*. An unfortunate title perhaps, but in a way justified. For Gottlieb *is* the scientific vocation. He had, inevitably, to be German. It was not simply that Paul de Kruif was immensely impressed by Jacques Loeb. To the young men of Lewis's and De Kruif's generation, science was German science, its embodiment the German professor. Gottlieb is a symbol not only of the transfer of European knowledge and techniques to the New World, but an expression of the peculiar mystique of German academic life. His worship of research *qua* research and his reverent attitude toward this pursuit of knowledge are very much the product of the German university. Such beliefs never established themselves with quite such intensity in France, in England—or in the United States. Yet the almost religious texture of this attitude toward the scientist's task is essential to the moral structure of the novel. It clothes Arrowsmith's long hours in his laboratory with a spiritual, an inherently transcendent quality.

As in the legends of the saints, every sordid aspect of Max Gottlieb's life is only evidence of his grace and a comment upon the tawdry standards of those who mock him. He lives in a "small brown weedy" house, rides to his laboratory on an ancient and squeaky bicycle, and wears the shabby topcoat of a poor professor. Most Americans could only regard him as something of a crank. His was "no work for the tall man at a time when heroes were building bridges, experimenting with Horseless Carriages, writing the first of the poetic Compelling Ads, and selling miles of calico and cigars." Yet on the crowded desk in Gottlieb's little bungalow, letters from the "great ones" of Europe awaited his reply—and mocked the collective wisdom of Mohalis and Wheatsylvania and Sauk Centre. But Arrowsmith is vouchsafed the grace to understand and find inspiration in Max Gottlieb's life and ideas. Arrowsmith too shares something of his curiosity, something of his indignation at the shoddy and imprecise.

Sinclair Lewis created Max Gottlieb, but with raw materials provided by Paul de Kruif. Gottlieb, De Kruif later recalled, was an amalgam of Frederick G. Novy and Jacques Loeb. Novy was the austere and scientifically elegant professor of bacteriology at the University of Michigan who introduced De Kruif to biological research. Loeb was his idol at the Rockefeller Institute. Though Gottlieb is a bacteriologist and immunologist like Novy, not a general physiologist like Loeb, his personality and mannerisms obviously represent the novelist's rendering of the articulate and sardonic German—or at least the picture of him which De Kruif had presented to Lewis. In his recently published memoir, Paul de Kruif describes Gottlieb as a "muddy mélange" of Novy and Loeb. There is little evidence, however, of his having been dissatisfied with this sentimentally didactic figure when, in 1924, he first read the manuscript of *Arrowsmith*.

The genuine scientists in *Arrowsmith*, Gottlieb, Terry Wickett and Arrowsmith himself, all share the same conception of truth. It is knowledge obtained in rigidly controlled experiments, knowledge analyzed and expressed in quantitative terms. There is only one assurance in life, Gottlieb warns the youthful Arrowsmith: "in this vale of tears there is nothing certain but the quantitative method." Though many biologists today would approve such methodological sentiments, they would hardly express them with such passionate conviction. Our contemporaries are almost a century removed from the philosophical preoccupations which meant so much in Jacques Loeb's youth. The emotional intensity with which he, and his fictional counterpart Max Gottlieb, express such quantitiative goals is clearly the reflection of an ancient conflict within the scientific community. This is the struggle between vitalism and mechanism.

Physical chemistry and mathematics were more than a method to Jacques Loeb; they were his reason for becoming a biologist. He had, he recalled, read Schopenhauer and Eduard von Hartmann as a very young man. And while a student of philosophy at Berlin, the problem of free will seemed to him the most central of intellectual concerns. Loeb soon found himself unable to accept the existence of such individual freedom. Nor could he accept the techniques of philosophical analysis traditionally employed in the discussion of such problems. Loeb turned to physiological research in an attempt to prove that animal behavior was simply the sum of inorganic phenomena no different in kind from those studied by the physical scientist. Human behavior too, he believed, was no more nor less than the product of such physical and chemical forces. The "mystical" aspects of life were to be dissolved in the acid of mathematics and physical chemistry.

Naturphilosophie had been thoroughly vanquished by the late 1840s; yet the struggle against it had left a lasting impression on German biological thought. The men most articulate in opposing formal idealism were imbued with an instinctive sensitivity to philosophical implications and many embraced mechanistic materialism with an absolutist zeal inevitably paralleling the idealistic convictions of an earlier generation. It was this period of conflicting ideologies which shaped Loeb's intense and consistently generalizing mind.

Jacques Loeb was, for example, an assistant of Adolf Fick. Fick was one of the greatest of Carl Ludwig's students and perhaps the one most inclined toward the study of physiological processes in physical and mathematical terms. And Ludwig—with his great colleagues Helmholtz, du Bois-Reymond and Brücke—had been a leader in the struggle against a romantic or purely descriptive biology. Loeb himself always regarded the significance of his classic experiments on artificial parthenogenesis "to be the fact that they transfer the problem of fertilization from the realm of morphology into the realm of physical chemistry." His earlier investigations of animal tropisms were, he explained, crucial because they proved that animal movements were regulated "by the law of mass action." (Max Gottlieb remarks to Arrowsmith when the young man arrives at McGurk, that he hopes "to bring immunity reactions under the mass action law.") When Gottlieb feels that Arrowsmith has learned the elementary principles of his trade, he warns that true scientific competence requires a knowledge of higher mathematics and physical chemistry. "All living things are physico-chemical," he points out to his disciple; "how can you expect to make progress if you do not know physical chemistry, and how can you know physical chemistry without much mathematics?" Arrowsmith's maturity as a scientist comes only in the last few pages of the book. His papers are praised in Paris and Brussels and Cambridge. But the socially impeccable Dr. Holabird is simply bewildered. "What," he asks, did Arrowsmith "think he was anyway—a bacteriologist or a biophysicist?"

In a very real sense, the values which sanction and direct Arrowsmith's quest for truth reflect those of Jacques Loeb and of a generations-old debate within the academic confines of German biology. As I have suggested, moreover, Max Gottlieb's values record accurately the laboratory scientist's impatience with the impressionistic and empirical aspects of clinical medicine. The physician could not, in the nature of things, be truly a scientist. The essence of medicine is the functional relationship which the individual physician bears to his patient. It is his task to heal—or at least to console. It is the scientist's task to understand. At best, De Kruif argued in 1922, the physician is a skilled technician of applied science. The attempt to train each practitioner as a scientist was simply delusive; a return to the preceptorial system of medical education would be preferable. Lewis too found it natural to accept the pure scientist's vocation as a higher one. The very social necessity which created the medical profession tied it to the exigencies of everyday life, to compromise and commercialism, to the collection of bills and the lancing of boils. As able, self-sacrificing and understanding as the best physician might be, he could never transcend the social relationships which formed the fabric of his professional existence. And to Lewis the essence of heroism, the gauge of a man's stature, lay in the extent to which he was able to disengage himself from the confining pressures of American society. His heroic protagonist had to be a scientist; he could not be a physician. And certainly not an American physician.

Both De Kruif and Lewis agreed that American society had debased even the pursuit of science. For both men the essential factor in scientific progress was the initiative and creativity of the individual investigator. There seemed increasingly little provision for such individualism in twentieth-century America. To De Kruif, no development within American science was more dangerous than its growing "barrack spirit." Centralization and bureaucratization of scientific research were not simply the inevitable concomitants of an increasing complexity within society and within the body of scientific knowledge—they were developments inimical to the impulse of spontaneous creativity. Hence Lewis's acid portraits of Rippleton Holabird, of A. De Witt Tubbs and of his League of Cultural Agencies. ("If men like Koch and Pasteur only had such a system," Tubbs bubbles to Martin, "how much more *scope* their work might have had! Efficient universal *cooperation*— that's the thing in science today—the time of this silly jealous, fumbling individual research has gone by.") The young scientist, in an unfortunate image of De Kruif's, was to be denied the "privilege of wandering forth equipped only with the rifle of his intelligence, and thus to remain for long periods of lawless and impudent penetration of the forests and jungles of ignorance." No great man had ever drawn his inspiration from the memo pad of a research coordinator. Their hypotheses, De Kruif argued, were drawn directly from the observation of natural phenomena. The investigator who sought his inspiration in a library could hardly be considered a scientist at all.

Jacques Loeb was fond of aphorisms. He was especially fond of one coined by his friend and teacher, that great botanist Julius von Sachs. "All originality," Sachs observed, "comes from reading." Loeb was acutely conscious of history and of the communal nature of the scientific endeavor. He might mock the institutions of science and the mediocrities who so often found shelter within such institutional bulwarks, but he realized the futility of rejecting the scientific community as such. He died full of honors on the staff of the Rockefeller Institute. J. H. Northrop, model for Terry Wickett, even though a lover of the outdoors, always maintained his academic connections. Neither Loeb nor Northrop was a failure; neither renounced the corruptions of academic science and both learned to live with success. Even the criticisms and preoccupations of the restless Paul de Kruif were, as I hope to have shown, themselves characteristic products of the intellectual and institutional history of the biological and medical sciences. The conclusion of *Arrowsmith* is not only an indictment of the handicaps placed in the scientist's path by American society, it is a rejection at the same time of the scientific community whose values justify this indictment.

The novels of Sinclair Lewis are peopled with the wistful figures of Americans whose spiritual potentialities are unfulfilled. Arrowsmith is a conspicuous exception. Paul Riesling in *Babbitt* and Frank Shallard in *Elmer Gantry*, for example were gifted with something of the sensitivity granted Arrowsmith. But unlike him, neither was able to enter a vocation in which his spiritual endowments could find expression. Their inability to conform brought only their own destruction. The tragedy of George Babbitt lies in the pathetic and overwhelming defeat administered his vague idealism by the forces of organized Zenith. In the scientist's life, however, such chronic questionings find a recognized social function. Even Arrowsmith's social inadequacies, his lack of humor, his callousness toward the old and the lonely and the workingman are simply evidences of his spiritual stature. It is the small people who make good administrators, who are attuned enough to the petty circumstances of life to function successfully within them.

It is this pervading air of compromise which finally drives Arrowsmith from his wife, from his child and from his laboratory in New York. His ultimate rejection of society and its demands has been criticized as callow romanticism—and perhaps it is. But it is the logical result of Lewis's desire to depict greatness and his inability to conceive of its being allowed to exist within American society.

DANIEL R. BROWN

Lewis's Satire—A Negative Emphasis

"To write satire is to perform a miracle. One must hate the world so much that one's hatred strikes sparks, but one must hate it only because it disappoints one's invincible love of it." This quotation from Rebecca West describes the essential motivation of the satirist, and it further captures one of the most intriguing facts about the satire of Sinclair Lewis—that is, the characteristic ambivalence toward his subject matter, a paradoxical love and hate for the things he made fun of. It was his satires that made Lewis the most notorious author in the world during his lifetime. What his indignant critics did not see or did not admit was that Lewis not only loved the sinners despite their sins, but actually, much of time, loved the sins as well. If Lewis retains any stature in American literature, it will rest on his satire, which is the essence of his world view. An examination of his satirical approach will clarify some misconceptions which have arisen from looking at his novels separately.

The satirical writer must give the impression that he knows what is right and that certain behavior is subject to ridicule. He also takes for granted that his readers side with him in castigating deviations from an accepted code. What distinguishes the satirist from the preacher, who also assumes a moral elevation, is the amusement, perhaps even hearty laughter, that is experienced at the expense of the revealed folly or evil. Most of Lewis's assaults were upon standardization, religious provinciality, narrow-mindedness, and hypocrisy. The illiberality he exposed has not disappeared from

From *Renascence: Essays on Values in Literature* 18, no. 2 (Winter 1966). © 1966 by the Catholic Renascence Society, Inc.

the United States. Racial and religious bigotry, puritanical viciousness, business cheating and duplicity have not vanished. It is a serious mistake to dismiss Lewis's novels as charming and quaint books filled with interesting, if out-dated, thoughts of American life. His novels give definite insights into the double-think of Americans of the second half of the twentieth century just as they did in the first half of the century. Lewis knew the ingrained habits of Americans very well. The warning in *Kingsblood Royal* about American racial prejudice is overstated, yet [the] observation is depressingly accurate. Many Americans believe—and probably will go on believing for years to come—that the Negroes are careless malcontents, rhythmical in an animalistic way, who would be all right if they would only improve themselves by staying in their place. Similarly, the undermining of democracy by fascism, the name of *It Can't Happen Here*, is still pertinent.

The fact that Lewis's novels remain effective as propaganda shows that satire does little to alter what it criticizes. Seldom, apparently, does the reader see himself in the satirical portrait, for human beings have a remarkable ability to excuse themselves. Rarely has any satirist ever been influential in stamping out the vices he reveals. If changes do ensue after he writes, it may be that the satirist himself was an effect of the forces of innovation and not simply the stimulus. Satire will continue to be written because it answers the artist's need, and represents the historical situation.

Behind Lewis's slaps at society for its folly and wickedness lies a brimming optimism. Perhaps not all satirists hope to remedy the ills they render into art; some write just *because* they do not expect improvement. Lewis was aware that his fiction had little salutary effect. However, he went on scoffing and censuring because implicitly he believed that men should be told of their foibles. But not all satirists are so. *Animal Farm* and *1984*, by George Orwell, are so dark and pessimistic that the reader is left with a suffocating feeling around his heart. According to the assumptions in Lewis's fiction, reform is not a juvenile enthusiasm, man *is* perfectible, and ignorance is not his birthright.

Nevertheless, the overall pattern of his fiction is made more complex by the fact that he was not always certain of the things he disliked. Part of the paradox in his work is due to a steady, discernible ambivalence in his attitude toward many of the ideas and characters that he satirized. He always despised certain kinds of thinking and actions, cruelty and coarseness of speech, for example, but his attitude varied from novel to novel. If someone read only *Babbitt*, for example, he would not experience the breadth of Lewis's hatreds. For *Babbitt* is only one of Lewis's moods. If the reader catches him in another one, say in *Dodsworth* or *The Prodigal Parents*, it is very likely that he will see how much Lewis admired the "steadiness" and basic good sense of the upper-middle-class businessman. Furthermore, in one book Lewis praises liberalism; in another he makes fun of it. He ridicules Babbitt for lacking a sense of beauty; he smiles benignly on Doremus Jessup or Arrowsmith for the same weakness. Sometimes he ridicules the Communists with scorn, and at other times he singles them out for commendation.

His satire is at its best, its most exciting, when he is totally armed as an opponent, as he is in *It Can't Happen Here* and *Elmer Gantry*. In these novels, he is undoubtedly one-sided and unfair, but all satire is this way. When the attitude becomes inconsistent, it becomes watery and tepid. Even *Main Street* and *Babbit* lack directness and cohesion because of the author's ambivalent emotions toward his protagonists. His ambivalence could have heightened and deepened his novels but too often the ambivalence is uncontrolled, arising from uncertainty rather than subtlety. In addition, the novels offer a norm within themselves against which to judge the action. Because he provides no adequate alternatives to their lives, the characters scurry around pursued by Lewis's scourge, but presented with no escape. Babbitt flees from his stultifying business world, but the "Bunch" to which he turns, Lewis implies, is just as arid and stifling. If Babbitt attempts to find a mentor in Sir Gerald Deak, all he discovers is himself writ large, elevated to the British aristocracy. Carol Kennicott's plans for a better Gopher Prairie are formless, since she is naive, and no one in the book serves the author's answer. One is left with the conclusion that Lewis's own solutions were formless. Moreover, if Carol Kennicott did prevail over her environment, judging from what one knows about Lewis's ambivalence, one might suppose that he would begin to censure her for her affectations. The net result of his uncertainty is that the reader, once he has stopped laughing, is left grasping for some standard of comparison with which to identify. Even when he does provide alternatives to the dreary lives and anesthetizing aestheticism of his characters, the merely exotic becomes the desirable, for no doubt Lewis was a sentimentalist. Usually all he offers as substitutes to a humdrum existence are Persian marketplaces, idyllic campsites, fairy girls, and jeweled roads to Samarkand. Certainly his travels throughout the world must have convinced him that such mystery and romance exist only in myth, or that they are, at best, transitory enjoyments. Perhaps the multiplicity of his trips demonstrates that he could not find in life the alternatives he created for his characters. His satire suffers most when, because he cannot provide legitimate substitutes, he throws sugar on the wounds he inflicts instead of salt.

Like all satirists, Lewis's animosities are more tangible than his loves.

Just what he wanted for his characters is obscure. Unquestionably he felt strongly that people should be told that too many of them possess only a cheapened and degraded appreciation of beauty. He knew that makeshift shacks of hick towns, newspaper verse, and dull conversations are not the height of man's accomplishment, and he makes these feelings very vocal. Moreover, throughout his career he consistently opposed such things as racial intolerance, rich men's insensitivity, rudeness to waiters and servants, un-Christian Christian charity, and mores mistaken for the voice of God. Beyond these he went only into vague notions of something better. In general, Lewis approved of behavior which can best be described only by the nebulous word "moderate." He admired persons who fall somewhere between the excesses of an Elmer Gantry and the mental sterility of the citizens of a Gopher Prairie.

Perhaps all satirists write only because they feel a compulsion to complain about the way the world is. Perhaps they write because they feel a compulsion to seek perfection. Most people learn to ignore the inequities, annoyances, and the extremes of the world—if they become aware of them at all—because they are too concerned with earning a living or making an adjustment to their society. Sinclair Lewis tried to perfect his readers with his abrasive prose; yet he appears to have changed his mind when one of the ideals for which he was striving was realized. When the stringent puritanism he hated showed signs of declining, instead of praising conditions, he went to the opposite side and criticized the new freedom:

> For a century the preachers had wailed that most people were not people at all, but subhuman or fiendish, because they drank and fought and wenched and smoked and neglected the church. Now, since war-days, there had arisen in America a sect which preached just as earnestly that most people were not people at all, but subhuman or even Baptist, because they did not sufficiently drink, fight, wench, denounce the church, and smoke before breakfast (*Ann Vickers*).

Much of the time Lewis did not know what he wanted. If he had known more precisely or if he had longed for something more than an appreciation of a vague golden mean, he might not have spoiled his artistic perspective, thus dulling his effectiveness, by fluctuating from one side to the other.

When one tries to articulate Lewis's affirmations, one is struck by the shallowness of his approach to intellectual life. Most likely this flaw is related to the sentimentality already mentioned earlier; both of them springing from an inability or an unwillingness to probe beneath social manners and only the most apparent or moral weaknesses into the psychological dimension. He should have investigated the spiritual urge that moves men rather than just the more unpleasant consequences of religion; the causes of nobility rather than just the ugliness of hypocrisy. Almost always Lewis confined his world to the surface, the easily definable. Of course, it is this same superficiality that made him such a powerful propagandist. Still one wishes that he had been able to draw more heroes and heroines who are worthier— like Arrowsmith and Dodsworth—than most of the ones he created. Lewis was much more successful at creating characters that he did not admire. He was much more in command with pompous, stupid, meretricious, vulgar, nasty, and banal individuals than he was with the persons he liked. He thought that he admired moderation, but unfortunately he applied this to the realm of his characters' intellects as well. Thus a considerable number of main characters, like Carol Kennicott, Ann Vickers, Doremus Jessup, Fred Cornplow, Cass Timberlane, Neil Kingsblood, and Aaron Gadd, are all second-rate minds. Far too many of his sympathetic characters live in a cloud, protesting mildly at the ignorances and follies of the pettier characters, but rarely really alive, forceful, or even able to articulate what it is they believe in. Ultimately the fault is a serious one—that the protagonists exist on the periphery of the novels, never quite realized.

There are no significant intellects in his fiction. In fact, he seems to have preferred that his heroes be nonintellectual and only half-educated. On more than one occasion, he makes fun of people who start to read a book but who get no further than a few pages, but the men and women he loved are also guilty of haphazard reading and learning. They might possess a personal library, which Lewis will catalogue, but they seldom get around to reading very much, and their thinking is always restricted to one or two subjects. Furthermore, they never have anything creative to say, and thus attain their reality by reacting against and refusing to be like the minor characters. There are no conversations in his books between persons who are literate and sensitive and knowledgeable. When he presents an intellectual, or even a thoughtful person, he usually resorts to denigrating the characters surrounding him to thereby raise him up. In addition, one cannot even defend Lewis on the basis that one can use for a writer like Hawthorne, the belief in the superiority of heart over head, for Lewis distrusts emotion equally, and the result is a series of heroes and heroines who contribute nothing to Lewis's reputation but embarrassment.

Perhaps the very nature of satire restricts the presentation in fiction of highly intelligent ideas of profound men and women. First, of necessity it deals with flaws, vices, and weaknesses in human beings, and not with their greatness. Second, satire always demands a suspension of subtleties for its effectiveness. When the satirist begins to show mitigating ambiguities in the ideas of people he ridicules, he makes his characters appear less foolish and evil, he lessens his and his readers' right to be indignant about folly. Writers choose another mode than the satirical in order to treat deeper topics. *The Prodigal Parents, Bethel Merriday,* and *The God-Seeker* show that Lewis without satire, without anger, has the intellectual penetration of a Hollywood "B" movie.

Not only does Lewis have difficulty with the intellectual, but at times he is clearly anti-intellectual. The novel that shows this attitude most obviously is *The Prodigal Parents,* a cartoon, in which Lewis defends all the Fred Cornplows of the world, who, as the author himself says, are sometimes named Babbitt. Fred Cornplow is Babbitt seen from his own point of view; he is mediocrity venerated. He does not even have Dodsworth's striving for understanding of himself and the human condition. The theme of the book seems to be that men like Cornplow should retire earlier than sixty-five so they can spend their money to prevent their children from grabbing it. Besides giving approbation to his hero's self-complacency, Lewis displays a misunderstanding of and antagonism to psychoanalysis. He reduces Fred Cornplow's would-be psychoanalyst to a foolish incompetent, and makes the man out to be a stupendous quack. Undoubtedly Lewis's aversion sprang from his own limited experience with psychological treatment. While Lewis in most of his work deals with flat characters, caricatures, persons larger and smaller than life, usually he breathed into them enough credibility for their existence within the story, but in *The Prodigal Parents* all of the characters are lifeless, heavily rouged, wind-up dolls. Nowhere is the shallowness of Lewis's intellect more apparent than in this novel.

Concerning the variety of Lewis's displeasure with his victims there is need for some clarification. Walter Lippmann was discussing *Babbitt* alone when he accused Lewis of using the same perspective no matter what he is ridiculing—cigar lighters or business villainies. Actually there are more shades to his feelings than he is generally given credit for. At the top of his emotional ladder, usually closer to sheer amusement, are his objections to the unwillingness of many people to enjoy simple human pleasures, like smoking, drinking, dancing, and joking. He thought it funny that people try to crush out of themselves harmless, everyday joys. Nor did he criticize sexual immorality, *per se,* for Ann Vickers and Doremus Jessup and others are, if anything, admired for their sexual experiences. Other things about which he felt only mild concern include inaccurate news reporting and bad poetry.

Down the ladder, one can find selections in which Lewis shows himself more passionate. For example, he more than once drives home the point that the deprivation of natural urges, when unduly extreme, leads to gossip, to frustration, and generally to an unhealthy adjustment. He snickered at the fact that the denying and suppressing of biological realities by parents time and again leads to blatant participation in the forbidden pleasures. Lewis's feelings for the most part fall inside this category of involvement. It is the largest, the most diversified, and most fully documented in his writing.

At the bottom of the ladder, closer to sheer hate, is the third category. Sometimes he is highly perturbed, as he is about fascism in *It Can't Happen Here* and racial bias in *Kingsblood Royal* and about the viciousness of so-called Christians in *Elmer Gantry*. Actually he achieves a Juvenalian wrath when he unleashes himself upon meanness, physical cruelty, and viciousness in a self-righteous cause, especially when these things are held up as desirable. In the same line, when he looked at fundamentalist religion as practiced in the United States, he saw that it serves not to ennoble people but rather to shrink and wither their souls and force them to entertain prurient and ugly thoughts precisely because they do not reach true Christianity. The preacher, Elmer Gantry, the wolf in shepherd's clothing, unquestionably is the character Lewis despised most, and he despised him as the embodiment of the religious impulse perverted into monstrous iniquity, a scoundrelly, unfeeling hypocrite whose very soul is blasphemy. In such characterizations the reader can sense the paradox of the satirist's attacking vices with the same merciless brutality that he deplores.

T. K. Whipple in an essay on Lewis comments on the tone of his writing, calling it shrill and raucous. Yet there are examples in his works showing skillful use of the devices of paradox, antithesis, anti-climax, and irony. Obviousness is, in large measure, the quality that made Lewis's satire popular. Probably too often he bludgeons his characters to death when he might have, as Dryden said, decapitated his victims so dexterously that they would not have known it until they tried to move. Perhaps if there were fewer mangled bodies lying around, he would be taken more seriously by literary critics. Very often the way in which his blunted sword displays itself is in a too-obvious juxtaposition of ironic happenings. To take just one example, Babbitt, who is not a stupid man, fails to see the flagrant contradiction in the statement

> that if there's any one thing that I stand for in the real-estate circles of Zenith, it is that we ought to always speak of each other only in the friendliest terms and institute a spirit of brotherhood

and cooperation, and so I certainly can't suppose and I can't
imagine my hating any realtor, not even that dirty, fourflushing
society sneak, Cecil Rountree!

This quotation is typical of Lewis at his worst, his least deft.

Satirists can be more indirect, more adroit, but it appears that Lewis
was afraid that his readers would fail to realize he had killed his character
unless he shook the corpse like a terrier. Perhaps the general reading public
needs a guide, such as the author, to help it evaluate the satire it reads. This
is especially apparent with irony, as is shown by the comment of the man
who, after reading *Gulliver's Travels*, said that he didn't believe a word of it.
Certainly all satire depends for its understanding on agreement between
audience and author, and if the audience is uninformed or dull, the satire
may be read inaccurately. But so often Lewis destroys credibility by pushing
his techniques too far. *Kingsblood Royal* is a good illustration. The book suffers
immensely because of the author's insistence on driving home his message.
Everybody but one or two persons in Grand Republic, Minnesota, is fan-
tastically bigoted. Every minute is taken up with thinking of new ways to
insult and humiliate Negroes, and when the public learns that Neil Kingsblood is part Negro, it becomes hysterically narrow-minded and malevolent.
Racial hatred is quite prevalent in this country, but Lewis's selection of
details is contrived beyond the brink of believability. Elmer Gantry is also
an exaggerated creation, but here the focus is on the spiritual leper in a more-
or-less normal world, whereas Neil Kingsblood is practically the only rational
figure in an inconceivable concentration of intolerance.

Fortunately, there are places where Lewis controls his tendency toward
leaving fingerprints on the reader's mind. Subtlety is not unknown to him.
Now and then he tucks his tongue in his cheek and says something like the
following: "For the first time in America, except during the Civil War and
the World War, people were afraid to say whatever came to ther tongues."
In fact, from time to time one can even discover examples of understatement
as in *It Can't Happen Here:*

> There were horrible instances in which whole Southern counties
> with a majority of Negro population were overrun by the blacks
> and all property seized. True, their leaders alleged that this fol-
> lowed massacres of Negroes by Minute Men. But as Dr. Mac-
> goblin, Secretary of Culture, so well said, this whole subject was
> unpleasant and therefore not helpful to discuss.

This approximates Swift in its indirection, and it must be admitted that such passages are uncommon in Lewis, who more consistently damns his characters by straightforward, blaring diatribes and reprimands. However, an important idea should not be overlooked in evaluating the quality of his satire. Almost never did Lewis use the scatological, the obscene, or the taboo, like cannibalism, to achieve his effects. Swift's understatement can arise chiefly because he relied on his reader's ability to see the hideous discrepancy between his shocking subject matter and his treatment thereof. But ordinarily Lewis preferred to use the opposite method and gain attention by impaling his victims in a frontal attack. If he is often crude in his technique, it should be remembered that he is so because he chose not to be crude in his basic material.

When less under the influence of his journalistic background, his writing achieves the gracefulness, succinctness, and cleverness of a fine epigram:

> The D. A. R. (reflected the cynic, Doremus Jessup, that evening) is a somewhat confusing organization—as confusing as Theosophy, Relativity, or the Hindu Vanishing Boy Trick, all three of which it resembles. It is composed of females who spend one half their waking hours boasting of being descended from the seditious American colonists of 1776, and the other and more ardent half in attacking all contemporaries who believe in precisely the principles for which those ancestors struggled.

There are a surprising number of passages that can be taken out of context and quoted, for Lewis's use of the language is not entirely as barbarous as critical commonplace would have it, nor is it as awkward as that of some of the critics who would disesteem his style.

When he is too obvious, it is almost always because he wanted to club his subject without waiting, brooding, honing his prose. Yet when he was able to restrain his indignation and achieve aesthetic distance, he could be caustic and witty, fashioning many a stiletto-tipped sentence, without succumbing to his worst fault as a satirist—elephantine clumsiness. In *Ann Vickers*, he manages to maintain control of his topic and waxes eloquent:

> (Penology! The science of torture! The art of locking the stable-door after the horse is stolen! The touching faith that neurotics who hate social regulation can be made to love it by confining them in stinking dens, giving them bad food and dull work, and compelling them to associate with precisely the persons for associating with whom they have first been arrested. The credo, based on the premise that God created human beings for the

purpose of burning most of them, that it is sinful for an individual
to commit murder, but virtuous in the State to murder murderers.
The theory that men chosen for their ability to maul unruly
convicts will, if they be shut up in darkness, away from any
public knowledge of what they do, be inspired to pray and love
these convicts into virtue. The science of penology!)

If Lewis had more consistently been able to strike this delicate balance
between hate and artistic rendering of the subject hated, he probably would
be ranked higher.

Presently, the use of suggestive names for characters does not seem to
be particularly in favor. At least, readers appear to demand greater sophistication then simple allegorical names, such as Sir Epicure Mammon or Lydia
Languish. However, the names of Lewis's characters are one of the most
successful aspects of his satire and cannot be dismissed too readily. More
like Dickens than Ben Jonson, he used names which connote pleasant and
unpleasant connotations as against out-and-out descriptive names. Most of
the unpleasant ones depend upon the harshness and awkwardness of their
sounds to convey the mood intended. A list of some of them will demonstrate
the author's deftness in selecting what must surely be the ugliest names in
American literature: Chum Frink, Fatty Pfaff, Dr. Roscoe Geake, Waldo
Dringoole, Dr. Jat Snood, Bessie Smail, Adelaide Tarr Gimmitch, Senator
Berzelius Windrip, and hordes of others. As one can tell from this brief list,
the names in Lewis also hint at something distasteful in their meanings as
well as in their sounds.

In his *The Anatomy of Satire*, Gilbert Highet states that the monologue
in which the satirist lets a character bare his own miserable soul is a particular
type of self-exposure "difficult to bring off, and must be written by a man
who is both a skillful poet and a subtle psychologist; but when it succeeds
the resulting self-portrait is immortal." He had in mind something like the
monlogue of the Wife of Bath. Perhaps Lewis is not a terribly subtle psychologist and only a fair poet, but the most skillful passages in his satire are
indeed the monologues of pedants, crooks, bores, boors, ignoramuses, and
hypocrites. It is in these that Lewis is superb. His parodies are wonderful
distortions, ever so slightly exaggerated, of characteristic thought and speech
patterns that are so credible that the reader sometimes finds it impossible to
distinguish the parody from realism. At mimicry Lewis attains his highest
subtlety. Here he does not strain for effects. Rather, he strings together, in
almost imperceptible aggregation, the contradictions and nonsense that are
present in a great many people. In *Kingsblood Royal* there is a marvelous scene

in which the Reverend Buncer tells the part-Negro hero, under the guise of giving Christian advice, all of the practical bigotries and lies and play-it-safe compromises that the good churchgoer needs to know in order not to worry about inconveniencing himself with applying his religion to his life. Some of the speeches his characters deliver are remarkable self-parodies more potent because of the informational fictional framework within which they are set. The following selection is from one of Babbitt's lectures and is only one paragraph from pages and pages that Lewis produced:

> In other countries, art and literature are left to a lot of shabby bums living in attics and feeding on booze and spaghetti, but in America the successful writer or picture-painter is indistinguishable from any other decent business man; and I, for one, am only too glad that the man who has the rare skill to season his message with interesting reading matter and who shows both purpose and pep in handling his literary wares has a chance to drag down his fifty thousand bucks a year, to mingle with the biggest executives on terms of perfect equality, and to show as big a house and as swell a car as any Captain of Industry! But, mind you, it's the appreciation of the Regular Guy who I have been depicting which has made this possible, and you got to hand as much credit to him as to the authors themselves.

Similar peaks in Lewis are his mocking imitations of preachers' loveless sermons about love and tenderness, examples of mimicry that persist throughout all of his works. Moreover, he is excellent whenever he lets a coarse, slangy character expatiate, revealing himself in all his glorious boorishness, as Mike Monday does in *Babbitt*, as Enos Tillery does in *The Prodigal Parents*, as Ted Granitz does in *Bethel Merriday*, and as Clif Clawson does in *Arrowsmith*, the last man's conversation with Arrowsmith's second wife being the one quoted:

> "Well, look: What I wanted to know is: Is this going to be just a homey grub-grabbing or a real soiree? In other words, honey, shall I dress natural or do I put on the soup-and-fish? Oh, I got 'em—swallowtail and the whole darn' outfit!

> "Attaboy! I'll be there, dolled up like a new saloon. I'll show you folks the cutest lil line of jeweled studs you ever laid eyes on. Well, it's been a great pleezhure to meet Mart's Missus, and we will close now with singing 'Till We Meet Again' or 'Au Reservoir.' "

When Lewis is this good he leaves the reader breathless with dismay and rage and a feeling that something must be done—and soon—to obliterate such ignorance. If such characters seem extraordinarily vulgar to the reader, it is not because they do not exist, but because the reader's experience in human types is limited. His ability to caricature is probably what will keep for Lewis whatever fame he retains. It is a gift that few writers can sustain as regularly as he, and it is herein that his talent as a satirist is most realized.

Satire is not likely ever to die, since it springs from dissatisfaction with human beings and the ways they conduct themselves, and Sinclair Lewis quite possibly may have a revival if readers once again discover that he captured much that is wrong in American civilization.

MARTIN BUCCO

The Serialized Novels of Sinclair Lewis

Contrary Sinclair Lewis owed much of his phenomenal literary success and failure to popular American magazine fiction. As far back as 1910, while hacking in the dream factories of the East, this raw Middle Westerner brooded over his hometown and his alma mater—Sauk Centre, Minnesota, and Yale University—and yearned for fame and fortune. Restless and tormented, he seemed always out of tune with people and places. When not playing the role of medieval lyricist or prairie euphuist, he contributed to the slow displacement of good fiction in magazines by cynically turning out, as he once confessed, "a swell piece of cheese to grab off some easy gravy." But what editors of the big slicks balked at, many literary critics admired; and what the critics denounced, magazine editors praised.

Nowhere is Sinclair Lewis's split sensibility more visible than in a collation of his serials and books. In addition to casting into the Dead Sea of literary mercantilism more than a hundred short stories, Lewis also tossed in seven serial novels, later revised and published in book form. For $1000 and *Woman's Home Companion* ("Service to the Modern Home"), he potboiled in two installments the Pickwickian travels of "the Innocents" (February-March, 1917), his fourth novel (*The Innocents: A Story for Lovers*, 1917). When the *Saturday Evening Post*, which earlier had rejected "The Innocents" as too bathetic, bid for stories of American romance and adventure—of Horatio Alger types scurrying up the ladder of material success—Lewis rehashed three articles ("Adventures in Autobumming") based on his four-month tour

From *Western American Literature* 4, no. 1 (Spring 1969). © 1969 by the Western Literature Association.

of the American West in a Model T Ford and sold his four-part serial, "Free Air" (May 31–June 21, 1919), and its two-part sequel, "Danger—Run Slow" (October 18–25, 1919); both constituted the frame for his fifth novel (*Free Air*, 1919) and the inspiration for his unserialized *Main Street* (1920). To *Designer and the Woman's Magazine* the now famous writer sold for $50,000 his shorter version of the modern pioneer spirit in eleven installments of "Dr. Martin Arrowsmith" (June 1924–April 1925), afterwards published as Lewis's eighth novel (*Arrowsmith*, 1925). In 1926, for $42,500, the diehard magazinist answered the call of *Collier's Weekly* for more action and more obvious motivation with twelve installments of his shoddy Western Canadian melodrama, "Mantrap" (February 13–May 8), his ninth novel (*Mantrap*, 1926). After Sinclair Lewis accepted the Nobel Prize in 1930, he resolved to create in the Great Tradition; but, still composing with one eye on the serial market, he granted first publication and bowdlerization rights to affluent *Redbook Magazine*, (August 1932–January 1933), *Cosmopolitan Magazine* (May–October 1945), and—the wheel comes full circle—*Woman's Home Companion* (January–February 1951) for, respectively: his thirteenth novel (*Ann Vickers*, 1933), nineteenth novel (*Cass Timberlane*, 1945), and twenty-second and last novel (*World So Wide*, 1951).

Since their readers craved uncomplicated narratives, magazine editors consistently objected to the best thing in Lewis—his social satire. Nimble in the calling of pleasing the flesh-and-blood counterparts of Mrs. Babbitt, serial editors and author expunged the gargantuan sniping, lashing, carping, smearing, grumbling, and general denouncing. The trick: to alienate or to insult no one, especially middle-class Americans who admired middle-class Americans. For example, in Lewis's weary "World So Wide," with its soporific irony (American hero travels to stange land, meets strange woman, but in the end marries familiar girl next door), the *Companion* editors removed the criticism of America from the Italian point of view, the biting remarks from the expatriot point of view, and even censored the touring heroine's mild observation, for instance, that Americans in Italy are richer in their hearts than Americans back home who take themselves "so seriously selling whisky or lawsuits or college-alumni enthusiasm."

From the earlier *Redbook* version of Lewis's "Ann Vickers," the editors deleted nearly a thousand paragraphs and thousands of phrases and single words, most dealing with politics, religion, and education. The serial heroine is Wordsworthian, the book heroine Marxian. Ann's girlhood rebellion against Sunday School is not in the serial—not even so tepid a sarcasm as her listening to "a lovely elocutionist gentleman with black wavy hair recite Kipling at the entertainment of the Order of the Eastern Star." Little of

Lewis's anti-academicism taints the serial; *Redbook* readers never learn, for instance, that schools like Smith and Vassar are excellent because scholarship there is *equal* in rank with tennis. And since the literary taste of serial readers is above suspicion, perhaps editors felt obligated to blue pencil the suggestion that there are better American writers than Zane Grey and Harold Bell Wright—a pair who were outselling even such popular Western authors as Frank Norris and the writer to whom Lewis in 1910 had sold story plots— Jack London.

Since magazine publishers envisioned their readers as belonging to the "better off" middle class, an optimistic and cheery group that by income or interests typified American ambitions, editors automatically eliminated objectionable Lewisian details. When characters drank, swore, gambled, disrobed, confronted crudity or cruelty, discussed sex, or did anything contrary to the prevailing dictates of middle-class public morality, Lewis expected— in fact, made or suggested—alterations. Editors regarded the statements of Lewis's unreconstructed lady radicals much as editors today of, say, *Good Housekeeping* might regard the stream of consciousness of Joyce's Molly Bloom. Thus Lewis's serial heroes and heroines were conventionalized, especially their libidos. The sense of propriety of *Saturday Evening Post* fans in 1919 seems as quaint today as some of Lewis's dated satire. Not only did the *Post* not permit a comic figure in "Free Air" to dance around "in the costume of Adam," but it did not admit that the drenched heroine, Claire Boltwood, "stripped off her stockings and pumps" and that both she and the hero, Milt Daggett, "rubbed their legs with their stockings." Naturally, the serial Ann Vickers is forbidden unholy sexual alliances. And Jenny Marshland, who sports a lynx jacket in *Cass Timberlane*, is decidedly more aggressive and flirtatious than is her serial counterpart, who wears a Persian lamb coat. The student of American popular art understands what monologist Lowell Schmaltz (*The Man Who Knew Coolidge*, 1928) means when he pronounces *Cosmo* a repository of the "best literature."

But what editors of *Designer* and *Redbook* excinded from "Dr. Martin Arrowsmith" and "Ann Vickers" in the way of violence, cruelty, squalor, and sex reflects how Lewis often wrote in opposition to a large segment of the magazine-buying public—and then how, after heavy editing, he reaped from that same golden harvest. From "Dr. Martin Arrowsmith" editors and author cut out the grotesque medical school scenes—for example, corpses hanging by hooks. Although Lewis was opposed to literary obscenity, he used a liberal supply of "damn," "hell," and "God" omitted from the serial. In "Ann Vickers," hardly recognizable as a muckraking novel of penal reform, the serial reader is oblivious to the book's solitary confinements, whippings, bloody razors, foaming mouths, skull-cracking, lynchings, foul odors, flies, rats, roaches, slop, vomit, and other naturalistic tidbits. Nor does Ann even ponder accident, exile, kidnapping, assassination, starvation, poisoning, and rape. The hero, Judge Barney Dolphin, is not even involved in the "Queens sewer case"—just in "a certain case." The serial eliminates all allusions to bawdy, pornography, seduction, sexual intercourse, abortion, and childbirth. Indeed, any critical reader can point a just finger at the book's morbid sensationalism; but the serial does not even admit phrases like "the stirring of puberty" or words like "adultery," "precautions," "Wasserman," "prostitute," and "morning sickness." Thus Edwin Balmer, *Redbook* editor, confidently proclaimed Sinclair Lewis's latest serial as "the best of our time as long as literary records of America are preserved."

Yet whatever gaucheries the editors of popular fiction deleted from Lewis's serials, many thematic clichés remain—to inform even the great debunker's unserialized work. Almost automatically, Lewis champions the humble against the powerful, the poor against the rich, the adventurous against the timid, the idealist against the materialist, the romantic against the realist, the maker against the intellectual, and the country against the city. These "commercial" attitudes appear, often ambivalently, in all Lewis's books—from the second-rate *Our Mr. Wrenn* (1914), to the first-rate *Babbitt* (1922), to the third-rate *World So Wide* (1952). Especially conspicuous is the East-West theme, perhaps the central tension in Lewis's life and work. In pitting the elegant, class-conscious, confined East against the drab, egalitarian, free West, Lewis shrilly defended the West sometimes, but without conviction. Try as he might to love the virgin land, he never succeeded. None of his books evokes the sense of what, thanks to Max Westbrook, has become a critical truism when discussing Western literature: "sacrality." Lewis's view of the West is essentially simplistic, sentimental, and exterior. He renders humor, speech, and manner, but not soul, diety, or sublimity— not even in *The God-Seeker* (1949), his unserialized historical novel set in the Minnesota wilderness. If the hero of *Work of Art* (1934) happily manages a little Kansas hotel, and if the battle against tyranny in *It Can't Happen Here* (1935) begins out West, there is still, among other things to beset Lewis, the spectre of Grand Republic racism in *Kingsblood Royal* (1947). Ultimately Lewis's ambivalence means: if the idyllic West is antidote to the cramped East, then the cultivated East, in turn, is antidote to the blank West—and remedy for both is the open road—anywhere!

A new or revisited place, Lewis half believed, would make a new person. The old Cape Cod couple in "The Innocents" end up in Delaware, but in the book version they head West in the mythic manner, optimistically seeking self-reliance and the joys of village life. Beginning in the serial "Free Air" and intensifying in the book version, a raw Western mechanic learns the social graces as part of his crosscountry courtship of an Eastern socialite, while she apparently learns the meaning of democracy. The shorter "Dr. Martin Arrowsmith" sets the tone for the full development of the pioneer spirit when the hero's great-grandmother declares at the start: "We're going on jus' as long as we can. Going West!" In "Mantrap," Lewis, waxing ebullient over the Great Outdoors, drops his citified Ralph Prescott smack into the tradition of Raw Meat survival. And in his Nobel Prize Speech Lewis spoke of Theodore Dreiser's *Sister Carrie* as having come to airless America as "a great free Western wind" and Lewis then called for a literature of America "worthy of her vastness." Thus in "Ann Vickers" the Middle West town, unlike *Main Street*'s Gopher Prairie, receives Lewis's nostalgic approbation; but only in the book version does frustrated Ann declare: "I would be glad if some ranchman out of an idiotic 'Western novel' came along and carried me off." Also, in his novel of modern marriage, "Cass Timberlane," Lewis reidentified himself with the West—Grand Republic opposes New York City. So in "World So Wide" Hayden and Roxanna Chart return home to Newlife, Colorado, with new perspectives. In all these novels, however, the author's capricious overtones suggest private dubiety—as if he half believed that a new or revisited place would not really make a new person.

While magazinists, then, objected to Sinclair Lewis's social satire and to his naturalistic details, they welcomed not only his commercial romanticism, but also his electric improvisation. Originally Lewis wrote his contemporary Western novel, "Free Air," for example, as a four-installment Open Road serial for the *Saturday Evening Post*. But as he enlarged the tale for book publication, he advised his publisher, Alfred Harcourt, to advertise the book as "romance with dignity and realism." Meanwhile, so popular was the serial version that *Post* editor George Lorimer pleaded with Lewis for a sequel—an unprecedented request. Having already revised the original four installments for book publication, Lewis seized an extra $2,500 and the inspiration of the moment, made an about-face, and revised his extended book episodes as a two-installment sequel. The *Post* then published "Danger—Run Slow" four months after "Free Air," in appearance and in effect, had ended. How Lewis exploited the commercial possibilities of "Free Air"— how he *bridged* the sixteen issues between the serial's last installment and the sequel's first—is a classic of improvised swagger.

In a thousand words Lewis reestablished the last scene on the train, his hero and heroine traveling West to marital bliss. In the process, he reidentified Milt Daggett and Claire Boltwood, summarized the earlier four installments, and then made a strenuous effort to convince readers with moderate recall that the story of Milt and Claire, after all, is not really over: Just now she is "violently engaged in falling out of love"—for how can she introduce this poor mechanic to her wealthy Seattle relatives? The serialist speaks:

> She saw no way out—except cruelty.
> And so her story, which had seemed ended, was begun.
> The end of every comedy is the commencement of a tragedy. When the wedding bells have sounded their pink gayety and the author with considerable weariness and an interested thought in royalties leaves the happy couple surrounded by kisses and presents, and indicates that this is The End—then it is time for another author to creep in and reveal the actual story, with the tragedies of dull evenings and social slights and sickness and the loss of bachelor friends, with the drama of enduring loyalty and of pride in children that is so much more alive than courtship's tepid experiments, with the abrupt disaster or the glorious endurance of the effort, and all the deep sweet humanness of the trudging years.
>
> So now, when Claire Boltwood and Milt Daggett believed that their real story was the motor flight in which they had found the easy and romantic companionship of outdoors, this typical prelude of the unengaged young man meeting a disengaged young woman was over, and their real struggle with life was beginning.

To be sure, Lewis gave the book version of *Free Air* more "dignity" by purging it of slapdash serial absurdities, but this rediscovered bridge exhibits to a sad degree the cynical banality of our first Nobel Prize Winner.

Serial and slick-story engineering was so natural to Sinclair Lewis that even after he committed himself to writing masterworks in the 1920s he consciously or subconsciously appropriated the serial form. Thus both the serialized and the unserialized Lewis novel—that is, every book in his choppy social canon—displays a more or less compelling series of contracted flights, each flight concluding with a teasing, installmentesque climax or cliff-hanger. Like the picaresque novel, the serial's loose, episodic, linear structure encouraged Lewis to extemporize with aplomb. While this narrative method enabled him to preserve or to insert both germane and gratuitous blocks of social criticism in his book versions, it also enabled serial editors and Lewis to liquidate blocks of social commentary without impairing the story line. In the serial "Cass Timberlane," for example, the book's brilliant intercalary "Assemblages" disappear; in "World So Wide" both social critique and the sense of place are gone. This method of composition--of "doing up a subject"—natually plays havoc with structural and tonal unity. Because of his awesome reputation, however, Sinclair Lewis could defy a few stock serial formulas. In *Collier's*, "Mantrap," for example, he introduces his heroine not in the conventional first or second installment, but in the fifth; he sets his story in a familiar America, but then shifts to the Canadian woods: and he writes a downbeat ending. But all too often the free-swinging Lewis overcompensated for serial straitjacketing by pouring forth in fantastic language embarrassing melodrama and sentimentality. In the padded book version of *The Innocents*, for example, Mother Appleby acts even more improbably than in the serial—her change is revolutionary; and, ironically, it is in the world of commercial fiction where precipitant change is counted a blessing. Besides being more robust than the serial "Mantrap," the book version also is more sentimental. And although in serials good people love horses and dogs, the book *Cass Timberlane* has too many saccharin comments on Cleo, the family cat. On the positive side, early serial publication (besides gaining Lewis money and limelight) taught him to re-see his characters and to develop them for the more critical book reader. The Eastern shop owner in "The Innocents," for instance, sells only shoes; but the shop owner in the book version, a Middle Westerner, also sells Lipsittsville—five years before George F. Babbitt sells Zenith:

> "Aside from any future business dicker between you and me personally, I'd like to show you just why Lipsittsville is going to be a bigger town than Freiburg or Taormina or Hongkong or Bryan or any of the other towns in the country, let 'em say what they like!"

Drab Western scenes which Lewis added to *Free Air* for Claire Boltwood's edification prefigure similar scenes which Carol Kennicott views in *Main Street*. Thus, even if censorious, American popular fiction encouraged Lewis to direct his blazing camera-eyes on the contemporary American scene. Also, between serial and book publication, Lewis always tidied up or energized his style. Since decorous homemakers liked his swift, nervous, bold language in its lower and middle registers, the serials display fewer verbal acrobatics. For example, "traveling men" in the serial "Free Air" becomes in the book version "pioneers in spats." Although Lewis's lucid, flexible prose yields a range of feeling from the maudlin to the savage, his coarse diction and brazen phrase (like frontier inflation) never adequately renders interior nuance.

The man of letters and the historian of ideas, fascinated by the struggle of opposing forces in the human soul, must indeed wonder about this sentimental realist or satiric romantic. Like Charles Dickens, Lewis improbably managed at times to transcend his education in the conventions of popular magazine fiction. But was ever a major writer in hot pursuit of the American Dream quite so divided as Sinclair Lewis? In 1946 Frederick Manfred described his fellow Minnesotan: "The face I saw was a face to haunt one in dreams. If was a face that looked as if it were being slowly ravaged by a fire, by an emotional fire, by a fire that was already fading a little and that was leaving a slowly contracting lump of gray-red cinder." Was ever a novelist out of the American West quite so parsimonious and prodigal as Lewis? Were he alive today, shuttling between the Establishment and the Movement, Sinclair Lewis would give to these rhetorical questions a pair of fabulously contradictory answers.

STEPHEN S. CONROY

Sinclair Lewis's Sociological Imagination

Sinclair Lewis was a novelist blessed with what C. Wright Mills called "the sociological imagination," the capacity to see and be interested in the overriding dramatic quality of "the interplay of man and society, of biography and history, of self and world." Lewis was often accused of being a kind of social scientist, although usually the similarity noted was in investigative and preparatory techniques and not in quality of mind. Mark Schorer for example pointed out that "with Lewis, the subject, the social section always came first; systematic research, sometimes conducted by research assistants and carrying Lewis himself into 'the field' like any cultural anthropologist, followed; the story came last, devised to carry home and usually limping under the burden of data." And Lewis too recognized the assumptions which underlay most of his work; he certainly was aware that his habits of mind and method of composition resembled the habits and practices of the social scientist. Most writers, he tells us, when asked what form the first idea of a story takes, will reply that they think first of a plot, of a person, or even of a setting. But speaking of his own practice Lewis says, "Actually, these three are from the beginning mixed in your mind; you want to do a story about a person who, as he becomes real to you, dwells in a definite house, street, city, class of society." It is, of course, this view of the individual imbedded in a matrix of neighborhood, city and class which constitutes the basis of the sociological imagination.

The power that this matrix has over the behavior of the individual is

From *American Literature* 42, no. 3 (November 1970). © 1970 by Duke University Press.

enormous. The universal recognition of this fact leads many to conclude that the human individual is completely bound up and hemmed in by his culture. Yet somehow the human remains intractably human and stubbornly individualistic. He believes that he has free will and he acts on that faith; he often rebels, questions, and struggles against any confining force. The individual who does this is capable of becoming, in his own eyes at least, a worthy opponent of the collective will of society. The "interplay" Mills speaks of then becomes a kind of combat, a drama whose resolution is not always tragic, even though the antagonists are grossly unequal. The observer with the sociological imagination is one who is aware that this drama is being played out around him and focuses on it. He may be either a social scientist or an artist; the important factor is his view of life, not his professional preoccupations. Without question Sinclair Lewis's imaginative frame of reference was sociological.

Given the nature of the struggle occurring, the problem for Sinclair Lewis, as for any novelist of a similar bent, is to determine just what responses or alternative modes of behavior are available to the protagonist vis-à-vis his culture. It is to Lewis's credit that he anticipated the formulations of David Riesman and even went beyond them in at least one instance. Riesman too, of course, possesses the sociological imagination, with perhaps a more legitimate claim to it than Lewis. In *The Lonely Crowd* and other works Riesman theorized about the responses open to the individual and concluded that there were only three: adjustment, anomie, and autonomy. Adjustment means conformity to the universals of the culture and an acceptance of the narrow range of choice left to the individual. Anomie in an individual, on the other hand, is virtually synonymous with maladjustment. A characteristic of the anomic is that he is never able to conform or feel comfortable in the roles assigned to him by society since he rejects its traditional norms and values. The third possibility is autonomy. The autonomous person may or may not conform. He makes choices; he lives up to the culture's norms when it is advantageous for him to do so, and he transcends them when there are reasons to do so. Lewis depicts two kinds of autonomy, positive and negative. He realized that the man indifferent to the demands of his culture could use his freedom for either good or evil.

The major works of Sinclair Lewis's greatest decade may be shown to be the working out in dramatic form of these sociological insights. *Main Street* and *Babbitt* both show the sometimes painful process of adjustment. *Arrowsmith*, on the other hand, is concerned with a protagonist who cannot adjust, one who becomes ever more alienated as his life unfolds. Finally, *Elmer Gantry* and *Dodsworth* concern men who are autonomous in two different ways.

Carol Kennicott, the heroine of *Main Street*, is usually characterized as a brave young bride who struggles pridefully against the spiteful parochialism of a prairie village, but George F. Babbitt is generally thought of as a near-villain of urbanized conformity. Usually overlooked is their similarity of outlook and aspiration, and the parallelism of their fates. They are both unhappy and restless in the society in which they find themselves; they both rebel ineffectually, and they both finally become largely adjusted to their surroundings. There are differences, of course, but they are often overemphasized at the expense of more important similarities.

Carol goes through a definite three-stage process of rebellion, withdrawal from and reconciliation to Gopher Prairie. Her rebellion begins with her first tour of Main street during which she is repelled by its ugly drabness. She also overreacts to the general blankness of the town society and to the dullness of her new companions. She then overcompensates with almost frenzied activity, gives silly but lively parties, and takes up and drops many useless projects. The village misunderstands her vitality and rebuffs her efforts. Carol feels, appropriately enough, that the townsfolk have rejected her, and she also suspects that they are scoffing at her. This reaction of the town has a double-edged effect on Carol. In one way it deepens her rebellion and causes her to involve herself in a situation even further outside the town's standard of acceptable behavior; it causes her flirtation with an ardent young apprentice tailor, which could have led to public scandal and disgrace. That it does not is due, paradoxically enough, to the town itself, for she rejects the young man's advances largely because she has grown to fear Gopher Prairie. She has made the first step in the process of adjustment when she cuts off a personal relationship for social reasons. Even if her action is largely motivated by terror, it constitutes a recognition on her part (and on Lewis's) of the power of the society to control behavior.

When rebellion within the confines of Gopher Prairie proves to be either impossible or too costly, Carol takes a step toward withdrawal. Her removal to Washington, D.C., like her earlier rebellion, is paradoxically but a step in her ultimate adjustment. Washington's sophistication and refinement prove not to be enough to replace the loss of family and status. She spends a good deal of time planning someday to take her son back to the open fields and friendly barns around Gopher Prairie. Also, in Washington she learns that there are Main Streets everywhere, and as Lewis tells us, in comparison to some Gopher Prairie's is a model of beauty and intelligence. In addition she begins to see that there is a thick streak of Main Street in Washington and doubtlessly in other large cities as well, a truism which George Babbitt is soon to learn in Zenith. Thus is the way paved for a reconciliation with her village; her sojourn in Washington has enabled her to come to terms with Gopher Prairie. "At last," she rejoiced, "I've come to a fairer attitude toward the town. I can love it now." Her view becomes more than fair, even hazily romantic: "She again saw Gopher Prairie as her home, waiting for her in the sunset, rimmed round with splendor."

At the end of *Main Street* Carol Kennicott is at home in Gopher Prairie in every sense of the word. She has not been beaten into submission; she has decided to adjust. Her return home is the result of three factors: her desire for her son to grow up in what she presumes to be the healthy environment of the prairie village, her love for her husband, and her new-found love for the town itself. Near the conclusion of the novel Carol voluntarily gets into the back seat of an automobile with a woman friend in order to let their "menfolk" sit together in the front. This symbolic act shows her to be, all unaware, finally a true citizen of Gopher Prairie. Originally Carol had too strongly insisted on her individuality against the pressure of her culture. She engaged in a battle which she could not win on her own terms; she did not have either the personal force or the social backing to change the ways of the town significantly. She either had to continue fighting and paying the terrible personal costs involved, or she had to adjust. Adjustment of course spells defeat for her aspirations, but it is a peculiar kind of defeat, almost without sting. When Carol ajusts she is comforable in her adjustment; only occasional, and mild, twinges remain, and only for a time.

Babbitt's struggle is very little different from Carol Kennicott's. He too squirms uneasily under the pressure of his society, rebels against it, and finally returns meekly to conformity to it. There is one important difference between Carol Kennicott and George F. Babbitt; Carol comes as an outsider into Gopher Prairie, but Babbitt is a longtime citizen of Zenith. Carol reacts to the village as if it were an icy pool she had just been thrown into; her immediate and almost overwhelming desire is to get out. Babbitt, on the other hand, is immersed in his surroundings as in a warm bath. As Edith Wharton observed, "Babbitt is in and of Zenith up to his chin and over." Only gradually does he come to realize that something is wrong with his society and with his position in it.

The emphasis in the beginning of the novel is on Babbitt as conformist, although he has already become aware of some disturbing impulses. He conforms outwardly but he is no longer completely adjusted; he has vague dissatisfactions and is full of veiled rebellions and escapist daydreams. What finally sets Babbitt loose, what causes such a conformist to go so far astray, are the shocking events surrounding Paul Reisling's attempted murder of his wife, his trial and imprisonment. After the sentencing, "Babbitt returned to his office to realize that he faced a world which, without Paul, was meaningless." And so his rebellion begins.

When a conformist becomes rebellious, when he is, as Lewis says of Babbitt, "determined to go astray," what can he do? He can stray sexually, or at least try to; Babbitt's attempts to seduce first a neighbor's coquettish wife and then a tough young manicurist meet with little success. These episodes are the somewhat more shabby equivalent of Carol Kennicott's flirtation with a tailor's apprentice, and are no more meaningful. There is also with Babbitt, as there was with Carol, a complusion to make the rebellion known. Babbitt is impelled to make a public display of his disenchantment with Zenith, and his display takes two forms. The first part of his rebellion consists of an entanglement with the bohemian element of the city, and continues with an adulterous affair with one of its leaders, Tanis Judique. The second part of his rebellion is political rather than sexual or social. He publicly avows some of the positions of the liberal minority, defends "radicals," and refuses to join an organization devoted to the repression of dissent. Although the first part of his rebellion is more colorful, the second part proves more dangerous to him.

Carol Kennicott had skirted the edge of adultery, but was saved by her feelings for her husband, her fear of the town, and her own fastidiousness. George F. Babbitt at first seems to have none of these problems; he engages in open adultery without bringing the wrath of society down on him, perhaps only an illustration of the double standard, but perhaps also one slight demonstration of the somewhat greater sophistication of Zenith compared to Gopher Prairie. Babbitt's tawdry affair and his infatuation with the bohemian fringe are frowned upon by society, but they invoke no very strong sanction. Babbitt increasingly finds his relationship with Tanis Judique cloying, and her friends less and less tolerable. In the last analysis, ironic as it may sound, Babbitt breaks away from Tanis and "the bunch" because of his sense of fastidiousness; he too has in some small measure that element so outstanding in the makeup of Carol Kennicott.

Carol never really feels the full weight of her society's displeasure; Babbitt, however, receives penalties ranging from loss of business through threats of ostracism and even violence. To the Good Citizen's League he almost becomes one of that undesirable element, parlor socialists. He is informed exactly what the league has in store for him unless he changes his activities: "One of the best ways it can put the kibosh on cranks is to apply this social boycott business to folks big enough so you can't reach them otherwise. Then if that don't work, the G.C.L. can finally send a little delegation around to inform folks that get too flip that they got to conform to decent standards and quit shooting off their mouths so free." The threat involved in the last part of the statement is not lost on Babbitt; he becomes slightly paranoic and begins to feel that he is being spied upon.

Babbitt is a rather stubborn man, so that fearful as he is, he will not give in to these pressures. It would have been interesting to see how far society would have moved against him, and at what point he would have broken down. But Lewis is not yet willing to let the conflict between an individual and his culture work itself out. With perfect timing, Myra Babbitt is rushed off to the hospital for an emergency appendectomy. Her surgery and extended recovery give Babbitt and his clan a pretext for patching up their squabble. With his wife's illness, the hostility toward Babbitt seems to disappear. He is even given another chance to join the Good Citizen's League, and "within two weeks no one in the League was more violent regarding the wickedness of Seneca Doane, the crimes of labor unions, the perils of immigration, and the delight of gold, morality, and bank accounts than was George F. Babbitt."

Thus is Babbitt's conformist nature splendidly reestablished; once again he sinks into his culture "up to his chin and over." Yet, once again, like Carol Kennicott, he is not completely submerged. He is the adjusted man, but there is in him as in Carol a residue of dissatisfaction. In both cases it is displaced onto the next generation. Carol looks upon her daughter as the one who will win the struggle with the village culture, and Babbitt defends his son's life plan even though it is not very promising. Babbitt urges him to have courage and to do what he wishes to do with his life. To Babbitt as to Carol children represent the hope for a brighter future. This hope is, of course, the culturally approved way in which a defeated rebel may find solace. Lewis still saw this deferred and displaced gratification as the best solution to the problem facing the individualist in a culture demanding conformity. The bohemian response he had no taste for, and he still seems largely unaware of the possibility of real autonomy. There is in Babbitt no character with the requisite intelligence and force to make the autonomous response. All that is left is conformity, adjustment, and a vague hope for a freer future.

In *Arrowsmith* the case is somewhat different. The individual's struggle with the demands of his culture is dramatized as the struggle between intensely individualistic dedication to scientific research and increasing tempting offers of worldly success. Martin Arrowsmith receives offers of success or potential success of a material sort often enough in his career. When he decides to leave Wheatsylvania, he is reminded by his father-in-law of the great sums he could soon be making, is offered a partnership in the village drugstore, and is tempted by certain political office. In Nautilus, Iowa, where he is a public health physician, a banker offers to finance him in setting up a private practice, and in the Rouncefield Clinic in Chicago he is constantly told that soon he will be made a partner and be eligible for a share of rather substantial profits. Martin, however, is not to be turned away forever from his chosen goal of medical research. He fights his way on to the prestigious McGurk Institute in New York, but is soon disillusioned to find as much importance given there to appearances, income, and status as in Wheatsylvania. He has climbed to the pinnacle and has found it too corrupted by America's materialistic standards. There is nowhere else for him to go within the system, and so in final despair he drops out of society altogether to become a kind of scientific monk cloistered in a Vermont farm.

The alienated or maladjusted man refuses to accept his culture, often withdraws from it, and tends to isolate himself within an impossible dream-world. Isolation is a solution which cannot work, by virtue of the very lack of any meaningful interaction with an ongoing society. Sheldon Grebstein, however, maintains that "what Lewis suggested by Arrowsmith's withdrawal from civilization was simply a refusal by the individual to be bound by conventional social codes, mores, or patterns of behavior," and he goes on to observe that this is an expression of Lewis's fundamental optimism, for it proves that "happiness can be found in America." Only in a very restricted sense is Grebstein correct. If America is defined solely as a geographic entity, then *Arrowsmith* does prove that happiness can be found there, for the monastic cabin to which Martin ultimately retreats is located within the boundaries of the United States. But if America is defined in the larger sense of a system of "conventional social codes, mores, or patterns of behavior," then Arrowsmith does not find happiness there.

The ending of *Arrowsmith* leaves much to be desired. It shows that Lewis continued to avoid a logical working out of real social conflict. In earlier works Lewis could somehow modulate the issues so that a resolution could seem to be achieved in terms of something as simple as the relationship between a man and a woman. Thus both Carol Kennicott and George F. Babbitt are shown to be in conflict with their respective spouses as well as with the surrounding culture, and the individual-culture struggle is resolved by solving the marital struggle. In *Arrowsmith*, however, Lewis is pushed to some unlikely plot devices. He finds it necessary to kill off the appealing Leora Arrowsmith, for Martin could not have left her and maintained the reader's sympathy, and with her his hegira into the woods would be either pointless or impossible. But Joyce, his wealthy second wife, was a good representative of the society from which he felt impelled to withdraw, and therefore she could be left behind without being cruelly abandoned.

In this novel Lewis shows the conflict between the individual American and the demands of his culture becoming more serious, and the solution for the individual becoming more difficult. In *Main Street* and *Babbitt* he says that the culture is a poor one but that it can be lived in, and that the best, perhaps the only, solution to the struggle is for the individual to surrender himself to society's norms. But this is not the solution offered in *Arrowsmith*. Martin's withdrawal from society, no matter how romantic it seems to be on the surface, is an act of despair. Unlike Carol Kennicott and George Babbitt, both of whom look to their children's future for justification, Martin Arrowsmith feels nothing but dismay when contemplating his son's future and their relationship. Lewis tells us that "Martin was afraid of him, because he saw that this miniscule aristocrat, this child born to the self-approval of riches, would some day condescend to him."

No matter how it is viewed, Martin Arrowsmith's solution to the culture-individual conflict is an anomic one. He gives up family, wealth, status, and almost all human contact because of his devotion to medical research. In this particular instance, since both Martin and his alter ego, Terry Wickett, have highly marketable skills, there is a possibility that they can survive on a few hours a day devoted to economically productive work, freeing the rest of their time for pure research. But their solution is not one that can be used as a model by others in a similar predicament. For most people this sort of total withdrawal from society is not possible, except perhaps at the price of sanity. Even the conformist solution of a Babbitt is preferable to that. Perhaps Sinclair Lewis realized this, for in his next two books he examined another alternative—autonomy.

If a man is not adjusted to his culture there seem to be only two possibilities open to him. He can alienate himself completely from the culture—the solution Martin Arrowsmith tries—or he can become autonomous. The autonomous man is not withdrawn; he is detached. He separates himself emotionally but not cognitively from the culture, nor does he withdraw physically from it. Autonomy is the solution Elmer Gantry finds, for his aberrant behavior goes far beyond mere nonconformity. Introducing him, Lewis says "Elmer assumed that he was the center of the universe, and that the rest of the system was valuable only as it afforded him help and pleasure." No other Lewis protagonist has Elmer's colossal sense of self-importance. A man who can look detachedly at his culture and see it for what it is must be a person of much self-containment. Gantry's ego is such that his image of himself surpasses mere self-containment; it is so inflated that he views the culture as something less than it is in reality.

Throughout the novel Lewis emphasizes Gantry's lack of commitment to the realities of his culture by employing theatrical allusions. His pulpit appearances are almost always described as if he were on stage. "As an actor enjoyed greasepaint . . . so Elmer had the affection of familiarity for . . . the drama of coming from the mysteries back-stage, so unknown and fascinating to the audience, to the limelight of the waiting congregation." The conceit is carried out in great detail: actor, greasepaint, drama, backstage, audience, limelight. He gloats later, "Never had he known such sincerity of histrionic instinct." Moreover, Lewis does not limit the stage analogies to a description of Elmer Gantry at the altar. He points out, for instance, that Gantry is careful of his appearance by saying, "He dressed as calculating as an actor." And finally, not to belabor the point, Elmer on first meeting his millionaire benefactor, T. J. Riggs, cautions himself to be careful because, "He's onto me." Unless Elmer Gantry is not what he tries to appear to be, unless he is acting, there is no reason for him to fear that someone will get "onto" him.

Since he is such an actor, and because he is so blithely evil, Elmer Gantry poses problems both for the critic and for the social scientist who has equated the autonomous man with the hero. Elmer Gantry is obviously autonomous; he transcends the norms for the adjusted with a vengeance, although in the wrong direction. And he is surely no hero; the truth is that he is a villain—an *evil* autonomous man. This is a possibility Riesman and others do not explore to any great extent, the possibility that there can be, as it were, both negative and positive autonomy. Elmer Gantry is both evil and autonomous, but his autonomy is negatively charged, being both destructive and morally corrupt. If Lewis saw Gantry in this light, as no doubt he did, it is no wonder that he became more reconciled to "adjustment" later in his career. Lewis has been criticized for abandoning his satirical attacks and becoming an apologist for American culture as he grew older. In part he did so, and his change of heart or manner is understandable as a revulsion against the immoral antisocietal type represented by Gantry.

But Sinclair Lewis had not as yet exhausted the list of possible reactions of the individual to his culture. There is the possibility of another sort of autonomous man. In his next work, *Dodsworth*, Lewis portrays a figure whose autonomy is positive rather than negative. Sam Dodsworth, when first we see him, is a man living in the world of things as they are and not as they ought to be. Lewis makes of him a man who grows: a man who begins as a conformist, gradually gains perspective, and even with this new insight does not reject his culture. In the beginning he is what sociologists would call an adjusted man; he is comfortable in his culture. As he says of himself, "Why, I never thought much about America as a whole. Sort of taken it for granted—." This was his response the first time his American assumptions were challenged in Europe. Much later he is rather amused at his earlier naiveté, or rather, his earlier unthinking acceptance of all things American. He tries to recapture what it was that he *had* believed and says, "I suppose I felt that the entire known world revolved around the General Offices of the Revelation Motor Company, Constitution Avenue, Zenith." From the man who takes things for granted to the man who analyzes is certainly a great step; for Sam Dodsworth the step is a change based on the painful process of hard thought.

Dodsworth is an intelligent man, but he has not been trained in analytic thought; on the contrary, he has been trained out of it. The welter of his new experiences in Europe demanded cataloging, and the most effective way of doing this was by comparing these new experiences to familiar ones from home. It was not an easy process for him because it demanded that he think "almost impersonally," and "it was a new occupation for him, and he was a little confused." But once this analysis begins it continues almost of its own volition. As it continues it is rewarding but uncomfortable; as Lewis says, "All thinking about matters less immediate than food, sex, business, and the security of one's children is a disease and Sam was catching it." What he is catching will not make him happy, Lewis suggests, for the more one is aware of, the more there is to be hurt and puzzled by. Dodsworth finds his awakening not particularly pleasurable. Thinking about impersonal things like cultural differences leads to pondering for extended periods about them: "thus brooding hour-long, . . . thus slowly and painfully perceiving a world vaster than he had known." When an intelligent man begins to think, to ponder, to brood about his society and its relationship to other societies in the world, he begins to detach himself intellectually from his own culture. No matter how much of a conformist he is in the beginning, no matter how well adjusted, he most certainly will gain a certain amount of autonomy. He has gained aesthetic distance from his society; he is no longer immersed in it, and he no longer accepts its ways as given. He may or may not decide to obey any particular norm, for he now has freedom of choice; in a word, he is autonomous.

One sign of Dodsworth' autonomy is the critical attitude he takes toward the ideas of his old friends from Zenith. He can no longer completely accept their opinions on economics and politics, although he is not yet completely detached either. His objectivity at such a time indirectly reveals one way in which Lewis structured the novel. Lewis has Dodsworth's gradual awakening to the nature of his culture parallel in many ways his gradual awakening to the true nature of his wife. The paths of Dodsworth's awakening regarding the nature of his wife and of his culture are parallel but do not lead to the same conclusion, for Dodsworth ultimately rejects his wife but he does not reject his culture. Interestingly enough, when he returns to America he will return with a new wife, for although he has rejected a wife he has not rejected the institution of marriage, nor the other institutions of American culture. But it seems clear that he will treat Edith differently from the way he treated Fran, just as he most surely will have a new outlook on his society.

In the last scene in the novel Dodsworth and his soon-to-be-wife share an experience which captures in miniature much of what the novel is about: "They were dining at the Ritz in Paris, Edith and Sam, feeling superior to its pretentiousness, because that evening they had determined to return to America, when his divorce should be complete, and to experiment with caravans. They were gay, well dined and well content." The Ritz is symbolic here of European civilization with all its rococo gaudiness as compared to the plain honesty of American civilization, and as Americans they feel superior to Europeans, especially now that they have learned all they can from them. And the word used to describe their decision to return is "determined," which denotes here a conscious and fairly difficult act of the will, for now they have lost their innocence as regards their culture; they will see its flaws as well as its good points. And one of the good points is that in the United States Sam will find useful, craftsmanlike work in experimenting with camping trailers, for America is a place, as they see it, of experimentation and new beginnings.

Of all Lewis's novels of the 1920s, *Dodsworth* is the one in which his hero finds the most satisfactory answer to the demands of his culture. Samuel Dodsworth, a good man, will return to the arms of his culture, but he will be autonomous in it. He will not sink into conformity as did Carol Kennicott and George F. Babbitt; he will not indulge in romantic rejection of it as did Martin Arrowsmith; and he will certainly not cynically "use" his culture as did Elmer Gantry. Samuel Dodsworth will be as autonomous as Gantry, but his autonomy will be a positive one, for he will add to his culture and try to change it for the better. This is also Lewis's most optimistic novel of the twenties, for it shows him in good measure reconciled to his culture. He does not picture forced adjustment to, desperate escape from, or cynical misuse of the culture. American civilization can be lived in, Lewis at last affirms, if only one knows how.

With *Dodsworth* Sinclair Lewis reached the end of his greatest period. He had by this time used up all the possible responses an individual could make to his culture. He had used conformity twice, anomie once, and autonomy twice, or rather positive autonomy once and negative autonomy once. And so Lewis found himself in a dilemma perhaps without being aware of it. His imagination still continued to present life to him in terms of man versus culture, but he had exhausted the possibilties of fresh action for the individual. He was condemned by the sociological quality of his imagination to repeat himself as an artist.

Lewis tried two or three ways out of the dilemma he found himself in. At least once in his later career he forced his imagination out of its sociological mold, and wrote a historical romance, *The God-Seeker*, but it was a flat failure. He also tried what might be called reverse polarity. In *The Prodigal Parents* he made the society good and the individual bad; much more so here than in *Babbitt* he celebrates the conformist as hero. But the novel is an incredibly poor one; Granville Hicks with justice entitled his review of it "Sinclair Lewis' Stinkbomb." Similarly, in *It Can't Happen Here* Lewis leaped a few years into the future and altered American society so far in the direction of fascism that behavior which would now be conformist then becomes rebellious. *It Can't Happen Here* is one of the best of the later novels, but by its very nature it was a one-time performance. It pointed no new way out of Lewis's artistic dilemma.

Sinclair Lewis was, by the limitations of his sociological imagination, forced into repetition. *Cass Timberlane* is much like a middle-aged *Main Street*; *Gideon Planish* is a pale imitation of *Elmer Gantry*; *World So Wide* is an even paler copy of *Dodsworth*; and *Work of Art* substitutes an obsession with hotelkeeping for *Arrowsmith*'s picture of dedication to science. There are other novels, some of which contain echoes of more than one of Lewis's greater works, but *every* later book is repetitive in some fashion or other. The sociological imagination of Sinclair Lewis, grasping the cultural setting of American life, seeing the drama inherent in the struggle of an individual with his society, and working out in dramatic fashion the possibilities for individual response which David Riesman would later give names to, is responsible in no small part for the very real worth of the products of Lewis's great decade. But on the other hand, the limited nature of this sort of imagination is also responsible for the sense of *déjà vu* one cannot escape while reading Lewis's later novels; the reader has indeed been there before.

HOWELL DANIELS

Sinclair Lewis and the Drama of Dissociation

It has long been a critical commonplace that Sinclair Lewis's novels are seriously and sometimes irredeemably flawed. The quality of his prose is generally poor, he wrote too much and too quickly, and no writer of this century with claims upon our attention can have published so many short stories of such little consequence. The internal organization of his works frequently appears arbitrary or simple. His characters are often approximations to humanity, blueprints for human beings with the complexities of motive and behaviour reduced to the minimal outlines consistent with an effective credulity. Cumulatively, it may be held, his writings testify to an emotional immaturity, an intellectual imprecision and a moral fuzziness. Yet the best of his novels continue to find new readers, and since the publication of Mark Schorer's monumental biography critical interest has quickened.

Lewis was a baffling and often unappealing figure whose savage pilgrimage in the United States and Europe now commands more sympathy than it once received. Sherwood Anderson early detected in his writings a man "who, wanting passionately to love the life about him, cannot bring himself to do so"; even in the last year of his life Lewis could say that he loved America still for its promises but he did not like it. His personal appearance tended to confirm his symbolic status as an exile both from his society and from the normal affections of the heart. His eyes, we learn from Malcolm Cowley, were those of a fairy-book hero, who is "taken for an idiot, and mistreated by his elder brothers, and sent bare-handed into the world

From *The American Novel and the Nineteen Twenties* (Stratford upon Avon Studies 13), edited by Malcolm Bradbury and David Palmer. © 1971 by Edward Arnold (Publishers) Ltd.

to seek his fortune, but he proves the wiliest of them all." Although Lewis achieved a remarkable success and exercised a wholly disproportionate influence—John Dos Passos has referred to him as "a sort of folk hero of the time"—personal happiness eluded him. His biographer, entirely appropriately, was to discern in Lewis indications of the official cause of his death in Rome; paralysis of the heart. As a major writer, however, his career had been over for some time, for if ever a novelist defined a decade and in turn was defined by it then that novelist was Sinclair Lewis and the decade the 1920s.

II

In the 1920 census it was revealed that for the first time the majority of Americans now lived in cities. The United States had become an urban nation. The succeeding decade saw the arrival of megalopolis and a phenomenal growth in suburban living brought about as a direct result of the impact of the motor car upon American life. A phase of historical development if not the myths associated with it had come to an end. In his Nobel Prize speech Sinclair Lewis could criticize those writers who "chant that the America of a hundred and twenty million population is still as simple, as pastoral, as it was when it had but forty million . . . that, in fine, America has gone through the revolutionary change from rustic colony to world-empire without having in the least altered the bucolic and Puritan simplicity of Uncle Sam." But in his own fiction, which presented the national lineaments transformed, Lewis was unable to escape completely from the prevailing mood of cultural nostalgia. For, in response to increasing urbanization, a defensive ideology had come into being which ascribed to the natural state a value that was metaphorical or spiritual rather than economic. Inevitably, too, as a result of the high proportion of foreign-born Americans in the larger cities, this pastoral impulse contained within it a strong element of ethnic nostalgia. It is a theme that appears but tangentially in Lewis's writings, but in this respect, too, he reflects the spirit of his age. In making his vague affirmations in favour of nature, it is obvious that Lewis is participating in a general reaction against the complexities of life in an industrialized society. Within two years of the publication of *Dodsworth*, a group of Southerners was to offer new articles of belief in *I'll Take My Stand*, but this agrarianism had been preceded by the diffusion of a pastoral nostalgia among the urban middle classes.

The one specific work in which this nostalgia is empirically tested is *Mantrap* (1926), the feeblest of all Lewis's novels during the decade if we exclude the five-finger exercise *The Man Who Knew Coolidge* (1928). Very loosely based on his own trip to Canada with his elder brother Claude, it is the account of a New Yorker who escapes from the mounting horrors of urban life to the last frontier:

> The long trail. A dim path among enormous spruces. Overhead gold-green light slipping through the branches. Lost lakes, reflecting as ebony the silver of birch groves. The iron night, and in the vast silence more brilliant stars. Grim wordless Indians, tall and hawk-nosed, following for league on league the trail of a wounded moose. A log cabin, and at the door a lovely Indian princess.

The dream is, in fact, the "most blatant of all our American myths: roughing it in the woods!" The Indians appear as "undersized Sicilians," and at the door of the log cabin is not the princess but an ex-manicurist. As a result of his amatory and other experiences, however, Ralph Prescott achieves some sort of self-knowledge before he returns, renewed, to New York; but the most interesting development is the nature of his companionship with Joe Easter, his guide, who quite explicitly informs him that no woman "that ever loved is worth giving up a real friendship for." Even in the wilderness, it seems, masculine fidelities are threatened by the female. The situation is but one of several such examples of male chauvinism. In *Babbitt* Paul Riesling and the hero sneak off to Maine in advance of their wives and, of course, in *Arrowsmith* Terry Wickett and Martin finally pursue in the depths of the woods the scientific truths to the attainment of which woman is apparently an impediment.

Whatever we make of this particular scenario, in Lewis's writings there is certainly evidence of that recoil from the problems of life in a complex civilization that Leo Marx had noted, but the direction of the recoil leads not to the creation of a pastoral regionalism but to a strange and, with rare exceptions, quite unconvincing internal fantasy world devoid of any value except that of exoticism. Dissociation tends to take the place of a nostalgic impulse unable to find its correlatives in a particular region at a particular time. From the biographical evidence available we know that Lewis's childhood and youth at Sauk Centre was a time of loneliness, that he was denied kindness, that his physical appearance brought him unhappiness, and that he turned increasingly to romantic literature for compensation. The conclusion of his short article "The Long Arm of the Small Town," written for the fiftieth anniversary of his old school's annual, is apparently merely another example of its author's endless capacity for self-deception:

> Indeed, as I look at these sons of rich men in New England with
> their motor cars and their travel, it seems to me that they are not
> having one-tenth the fun which I had as a kid, swimming and
> fishing in Sauk Lake, or cruising its perilous depths on a raft
> (probably made of stolen logs), tramping out to Fairy Lake for a
> picnic, tramping ten miles on end, with a shotgun, in October;
> sliding on Hoboken Hill, stealing melons, or listening to the
> wonders of an elocutionist at the G.A.R. Hall. It was a good
> time, a good place and a good preparation for life.

Although he returned regularly to Sauk Centre, it was the town's prejudice,
ignorance and meanness that he chose to commemorate.

Instead of the concrete remembered values of childhood, Lewis's characters proffer the vaguenesses of a fantasy world that is often the adjunct of
youth. When Lewis began writing verse his subject—in Fenimore Cooper's
terminology—was the castle rather than the cornfield; as a student at Yale
his literary contributions were suffused with a thin, post-Romantic medi-
evalism; and even in his correspondence with the woman who was to become
his first wife he cast himself in the roles of Jacques the Jester and Francois
the Troubadour. In the introduction to *Selected Short Stories* (1935) Lewis
could disclose that "he, who has been labelled a 'satirist' and a 'realist,' is
actually a romantic medievalist of the most incurable sort." If he was not
quite accurate in his assessment of himself as "essentially a story-teller,"
there is no reason to doubt the truth of his acknowledging, in a self-composed
obituary of 1941, that "Mr. Lewis smote—or tries to smite—sentimentality
because he knew himself to be, at heart, a sentimentalist, a romanticist."

The effect of this persistent romantic strain in Lewis's imagination is
that characters, who generally speaking have no sense of history, must resort
to fantasy in order to come to terms with or escape from their society. They
tend to be individuals continuously in a state of self-creation, seeking a
humanity which their creator is perhaps incapable of providing. It is, therefore, not surprising that Sinclair Lewis has sometimes been criticized for
failing to establish a dynamic relationship between a character and the society
against which he or she is in revolt; instead, it is argued, there is substituted
an "outward acquiescence and inward rebellion that is the death of drama."
But this condition of dissociation has always existed as a permanent feature
of American life; its obverse is that urge to conformity in a nation populated,
after all, by immigrants who underwent the most drastic form of dissociation
when they crossed the Atlantic. At this point it may be useful to turn to
Mary McCarthy's essay "America the Beautiful" in which she maintains that

the "openness of the American situation creates the pity and the terror; status is not protection; life for the European is a career; for the American it is a hazard." She goes on to state that all attempts to introduce a concept of the "little man" have failed, for a national passivity should not be confused with abjectness:

> Americans will not eat this humble pie; we are still nature's noblemen. Yet no tragedy results, though the protagonist is everywhere; dissociation takes the place of conflict, and the drama is mute.

It is this mute drama of dissociation that is central to Lewis's best works of the nineteen twenties—*Main Street*, *Babbitt* and *Dodsworth*—and it is with these three novels that this essay is primarily concerned.

III

The little man does, however, make an appearance in Lewis's first novel, *Our Mr. Wrenn*, which is interesting for the way in which it anticipates the essential pattern of Lewis's better-known works—discontent, escape, compromise or defeat. Initially bludgeoned into acquiescence by his environment, the Wellsian title figure can only resort to his imagination to justify his dreary existence. Then, with the aid of a legacy, there is a physical escape—to Europe, as it will be in Lewis's last and posthumously published novel *World So Wide*. The dream landscape possesses the usual ogres; the head foreman on the cattle boat is known as Satan and there is one Pete, who "was very evil." The *princesse lointaine* is Istra Nash, an exotic creature who, as so often in Lewis's fictional world, succeeds in depriving a sexual relationship of meaning by reducing it to an infantile level. She refers to Wrenn as "Mouse" and to them both as babes in the wood. In a manner similar to that adopted by Sharon in *Elmer Gantry* and Fran Dodsworth, when this type of association is in any way threatened by more elemental feelings it is quickly restored by means of a special vocabulary. One is tempted to locate the motives for these extraordinary reductions of adult relationships in Lewis himself, but the presence of the same phenomenon in the writings of some of his contemporaries, including Hemingway and Fitzgerald, suggests a larger explanation should perhaps be looked for. In *Our Mr. Wrenn* fact finally triumphs over fantasy, and the book ends with the successful hero striding into a Babbitt-like future:

> "Gee!" he moaned, "it's the first time I've noticed a sunset for a month! I used to see knight's flags and Mandalay and all sorts of stuff in sunsets."

Wistfully the exile gazed at his lost kingdom, till the October
chill aroused him.

For all its flights of fancy *Our Mr. Wrenn* is set in a visible and verifiable
world; *The Innocents* (1917) makes no pretence to realism. Lewis described it
as "a flagrant excursion, a tale for people who still read Dickens and clip out
spring poetry and love old people and children." In fact, the novel is even
more sentimental than the author's summary of it, as the elderly Applebys
wander across rural America (and in the process become folk-heroes) before
achieving happiness and prosperity in a small Indiana town. It is a fairy tale,
pure and simple, an attempt to recreate in American terms the Golden Age
mentioned by Lewis in his introduction. Lewis's other novels to appear before
1920 were *The Trail of the Hawk* (1915), *The Job* (1917) and *Free Air* (1919).
All are variants on the quest theme set forth in *Our Mr. Wrenn* and all, in
varying degrees, hover between the depiction of the realities of American
life and a contrary tendency, seen in characterization and structure, to indulge
in the familiar rhetoric offered by the possibilities of romance. Of these the
most realistic is *The Job*, an account of a young woman's survival and success
in the business world of New York, and perhaps the most interesting *Free
Air*, in which Gopher Prairie is introduced for the first time. Where a number
of years and several hundred pages were necessary for Carol Kennicott to
come to an understanding of the town, here one night only is required. What
appears to be insupportable rudeness in the evening is seen in the morning
to be genuine friendliness. In this novel, however, and in its predecessors,
despite a similarity of themes, there is nothing to indicate that with the
publication of *Main Street* Lewis would acquire an international reputation
and add a new phrase to the language.

Main Street appeared in 1920, and is the great romantic satire of its
decade. Its heroine, Carol Kennicott, is, like Isabel Archer, an absolutist of
the imagination; they both exemplify what T. S. Eliot has called *bovarysme*,
the adoption of an aesthetic rather than a moral attitude towards life. Instead
of the airless study in Albany we are offered the cliffs above Mankato where
the valley held in and made coherent the dreams that in the prairie "go flying
off into the big space." This essential element in Carol's thought is made
quite plain as the train bears her to Gopher Prairie and is dramatized later
in a conversation with Vida Sherwin in which Carol claims:

> The civic improvements which I'd like the Thanatopsis to ad-
> vocate are Strindberg plays, and classic dancers—exquisite legs
> beneath tulle—and . . . a thick, black-bearded, cynical French-
> man who would sit about and drink and sing opera and tell bawdy

stories and laugh at our proprieties and quote Rabelais and not
be ashamed to kiss my hand!

Her romantic imagination derives its stimuli from and operates in respect
to two areas: the Europe of fiction, poetry and painting and the natural
grandeur of the prairie with its associated memories of the frontier. Between
these conflicting principles for human development Carol is caught in the
frozen historical moment represented by Gopher Prairie. In the opposition
between her and the environment she in turn invokes first one and then the
other of these imaginative possibilities, either in order to escape temporarily
from the stultifying society of Gopher Prairie or to impose upon it the values
that to her mind it conspicuously lacks.

Her reading of Yeats brings "the flutter of twilight linnets, the aching
call of gulls along a shore to which the netted foam crept out of darkness,"
but the prosaic reaction of her husband ensures that this is her last attempt
"to buy the lilies of Avalon and the sunsets of Cockaigne in tin cans at Ole
Jensen's Grocery." Indeed, so committed is the novel to Carol's point of
view that we can only guess that her imperfect understanding of "culture"—
a *fin-de-siècle* mixture of Yeats's poetry, Chinese masquerade costumes, Jap-
anese obi, Dunsany plays and dreams of Venice and Mentone—reflects a
similar limitation in Lewis himself. When, finally, she gives up the struggle
and decides to dissociate herself and her son completely from the world of
Gopher Prairie the fantasy, appropriately, transcends the actual and locates
itself in the never-never land of faery:

> We're going to find elephants with golden howdahs from which
> peep young maharanees with necklaces of rubies, and a dawn sea
> coloured like the breast of a dove, and a white and green house
> filled with books and silver tea-sets.

But the major role in the novel is played by the myth of the frontier.
Main Street is haunted by the consciousness of the past and a confidence for
the future. It begins and in one sense may be said to end with meditations
on empire. The classical opening—a figure in a landscape—sets the scene
in the present but it is a present heavy with memories of a recent past, too
near for nostalgia. Where Chippewas had camped two generations earlier,
Carol expectantly stands: "The days of pioneering, of lassies in sunbonnets,
and bears killed with axes in piney clearings, are deader now than Camelot;
and a rebellious girl is the spirit of that bewildered empire called the American
Middlewest." Towards the end of the novel Carol, having seemingly made
her peace with the town, is conscious that the prairie is no longer the empty

land she had once thought it but a "living tawny beast which she had fought and made beautiful by fighting." Across the continent it stretches, "a dominion which will rise to unexampled greatness when other empires have grown senile." The alternative possibilities can be expressed in social and political terms: if Carol cannot have the formal ballroom she prefers the puncheon floor and the dancing fiddler; she is unable to conceive of the future except in similar polarities:

> A future of cities and factory smut where now are loping empty fields? Homes universal and secure? Or placid châteaux ringed with sullen huts? . . . The ancient style inequalities, or something different in history, unlike the tedious maturity of other empires?

But Gopher Prairie is neither Europe nor the heroic frontier, and it resists alike the crude sophistication and false simplicity that Carol attempts to impose upon it.

There is even a certain amount of attitudinizing in her reaction to the natural landscape in which, intermittently, she finds the dignity and greatness that elude her in the town. Although Lewis in elegiac mood can evoke successfully the passing seasons of a distinctive regional landscape, the nostalgic impulse is blurred by rhetoric when it attempts to move beyond nature into history. One or two sharply defined images, such as those the Kennicotts encounter at Mendato, scarcely compensate for the basic failure of historical insight.

A similar indecision permeates Lewis's conception of his heroine's character, and this in turn derives from his own ambivalent attitude towards the civilization represented by Gopher Prairie. Although the book is certainly a venomous indictment of the stupidities and banalities of the small town, it is necessary to remember that the novelist and his wife originally explained that the work was intended to illustrate Carol's learning "the great secret of life in being content with a real world in which it is never possible to create an ideal setting." The epistemology of the novel is suspect. At one level the double standard is illustrated in the deliberate juxtaposition of the conflicting points of view of Carol and her future maid as they both survey the town for the first time: for the one it is a bleak nightmare, for the other a glamorous dream. At another level Carol's somewhat belated recognition on her return to Gopher Prairie that not individuals but institutions are the enemies would seem to invalidate the truth of many of her earlier criticisms of the town. It is, however, one of the ironies of history that the harsh angularities of Gopher Prairie, which so appalled Lewis's heroine, have softened with time and, with all the detail of an Andrew Wyeth painting, the novel now recalls a vanished innocence.

IV

"He is the typical T.B.M.," wrote Lewis, "the man you hear drooling in the Pullman smoker; but having once so seen him, I want utterly to develop him so that he will seem not just typical but an individual." To his publisher he added that Babbitt was meant to represent "all of us Americans at 46, prosperous but worried, wanting—passionately—to seize something more than motor cars and a house *before it's too late*." In his desire to make his character both an individual and yet representative of a larger group, Lewis seems to have been caught in a dilemma; since, as Edith Wharton (to whom the novel was dedicated) put it in a letter to him, "Babbitt is in and of Zenith up to his chin and over," it might seem difficult for Lewis to endow him with traits or quirks that do not reflect back upon or indeed take their distinguishing features from his immediate environment. He succeeds in his intention as a result of the decision to offer us two Babbitts: the gregarious realtor and the asocial dreamer, the complacent conformist and the ageing man who hears dimly the same voice that will whisper to Saul Bellow's Henderson. It may be a limited achievement but it is Lewis's only complete success.

Babbitt is the sole major figure in Lewis's novels of the 1920s who appears immediately before us in the full panoply of the self. During the course of the novel we learn something of his past life but in the opening chapters he is susceptible to a larger freedom of interpretation than Carol Kennicott, Martin Arrowsmith, Elmer Gantry or Sam Dodsworth, all of whom are in varying degrees introduced in terms of their background. Established at once, also, is Lewis's point of view. Zenith is presented as an enchanted city, a living organism, proud of its towers, disdaining its past:

> The towers of Zenith aspired above the morning mist; austere towers of steel and cement and limestone, sturdy as cliffs and delicate as silver rods. They were neither citadels nor churches, but frankly and beautifully office buildings.
>
> The mist took pity on the fretted structures of earlier generations: the Post Office with its shingle-tortured mansard, the red brick minarets of hulking old houses, factories with stingy and sooted windows, wooden tenements coloured like mud. The city

was full of such grotesqueries, but the clean towers were thrusting
them from the business centre, and on the farther hills were
shining new houses, homes—they seemed—for laughter and
tranquillity.

The one unconfident note—"they seemed"—hinting at a reality yet to be
revealed is repeated in the last phrase of this opening section: "a city built—
it seemed—for giants." The panoramic sweep then narrows to focus on the
podgy citizen-hero, Babbitt, uneasily suspended in sleep between the two
worlds represented by the dream child and the morning noises of Floral
Heights: "There was nothing of the giant in the aspect of the man who was
beginning to awaken on the sleeping-porch of a Dutch Colonial house."

In these opening paragraphs the sentience attributed to the city and to
the limousine that "fled" over the bridge is reflected later in the resistivism
of objects which Babbitt encounters in his daily routine; the new razor blades
that are misplaced, the oiled envelope that will not unwrap as it should; a
bedroom which, released of its occupants, "settled instantly into imperson-
ality." The list can be extended: Babbitt's office becomes his pirate ship and
his car "the perilous excursion ashore"; the office itself is part of the Reeves
building serviced by "little unknown people" who "were in no way city
dwellers" but mere "rustics"; a nickelled cigar lighter becomes "treasure"
and the car for which it is destined "an aspiration to knightly rank." Although
these examples suggest the nature of the relationship between Babbitt and
his environment, his attitude is made explicit as he drives home from Eathorne's house, where the chairs are "gently supercilious":

> The air was shrewd, the snow was deep in uncleared alleys, and
> beyond the city, Babbitt knew, were hillsides of snow-drift among
> wintry oaks, and the curving ice-enchanted river.
> He loved his city with passionate wonder.

And in some ways Zenith is as much the hero of this book as the resident
whose job it is to serve the city by extending and populating it.

It is this capacity for wonder, admirably sustained in a prose which
moves easily between Babbitt's world of fact and world of fantasy, that is
the key to his individuality. In himself a curious mixture of aggressive and
regressive tendencies, Babbitt's domain is essentially that defined in the work
of Lewis's contemporary, James Thurber, where man, menaced by organizations, machines and women, must resort to irrational forms of compensation in order to preserve his identity. Indeed, one of the reasons for the
superiority of *Babbitt* over its immediate predecessor is that the solemn Carol

attempts to inflict upon the community a programme of eminently rational compensation. Babbitt, whether in his pirate ship or facing unknown dangers with the fairy child or imaginatively transforming the plump businessman into a skilled frontiersman, is triumphantly Mitty-like in his lonely but persuasive irrationality. At the end of Babbitt's first day, for instance, we find him in his tub:

> The drain-pipe was dripping, a dulcet and lively song: dripetty drip drip dribble, dripetty drip drip drip. He was enchanted by it. He looked at the solid tub, the beautiful nickel taps, the tiled walls of his room, and felt virtuous in the possession of this splendour.
>
> He roused himself and spoke gruffly to his bath-things. "Come here! You've done enough fooling!" he reproved the treacherous soap and defied the scratchy nail-brush with "Oh you would, would you!" He soaped himself, and rinsed himself, and austerely rubbed himself; he noted a hole in the Turkish towel, and meditatively thrust a finger through it, and marched back to his bedroom, a grave and unbending citizen.
>
> There was a moment of gorgeous abandon, a flash of melodrama such as he found in traffic-driving, when he laid out a clean collar, discovered that it was frayed in front, and tore it up with a magnificent yeeeeeing sound.

The extravagant language is obviously employed for satiric purposes in drawing to a close this hyperbolic description of the Babbitt day; but at a deeper level the responses evoked tend to contradict the ironic drift for they complicate our reaction to Babbitt himself in so far as a warm affection for him is both reflected and generated.

For Babbitt is trapped in the conflict between his private and public self, between on the one hand the demands of his business and an oppressive feminism ("a restricted region of wives and stenographers, and of suggestions not to smoke so much") and on the other a deeply-felt if unarticulated need to express his concealed self. The opportunities for this are few, but one such occurs when the Zenith delegation makes its bid for the next realtor's convention:

> At the head [of the procession] was big Warren Whitby, in the bearskin and gold-and-crimson coat of a drum-major. Behind him, as a clown, beating a bass drum, extraordinarily happy, was Babbitt.

Babbitt is the facsimile of an adult. The objects in his suit, which to him "were of eternal importance, like baseball or the Republican Party," confirm his status but the manner of presentation suggests they are indices to a reality of which he is never quite sure:

> They included a fountain pen and a silver pencil (always lacking a supply of new leads) which belonged in the right-hand upper vest pocket. Without them he would have felt naked. On his watch-chain were a gold pen-knife, silver cigar-cutter, seven keys (the use of two of which he had forgotten), and incidentally a good watch. Depending from the chain was a large, yellowish elk's tooth—proclamation of his membership in the Benevolent and Protective Order of Elks. Most significant of all was his loose-leaf pocket note-book, that modern and efficient note-book which contained the addresses of people whom he had forgotten, prudent memoranda of postal money-orders which had reached their destinations months ago, stamps which had lost their mucilage, clippings of verses by T. Cholmodeley Frink and of the newspaper editorials from which Babbitt got his opinions and his polysyllables, notes to be sure and do things which he did not intend to do, and one curious inscription—D.S.S.D.M.Y.P.D.F.

His theology is as confused and boyish as the contents of his pockets. After his rebellion is over Babbitt cautiously checks on the prospects of salvation, but this is hardly surprising since to him heaven was "rather like an excellent hotel with a private garden."

The act of dissociation assumes different forms in the novel. Babbitt, as the point of view makes clear, is in one sense already at a remove from the "realities" of Zenith; he exists in a state of perilous equilibrium between himself and his environment. Throughout the book, too, the woods of Maine occur as a leitmotif. There, with Paul Riesling, Babbitt "revelled in a good sound dirtiness" as in a mood of truancy he exposes his body and troubled spirit to a conventional immersion in nature. Even after the wives have appeared, bringing with them matriarchal prohibitions and restrictions, he feels as though "he had cleansed his veins of poisonous energy and was filling them with wholesome blood." But the solution is temporary; Maine eventually fails him and Babbitt has one of his rare moments of insight when he realizes that he cannot run away from himself. Dissociation then becomes open revolt as he rebels against the tyranny of marriage and the depotism of the standardized beliefs that he had earlier defended in his speech to the Zenith Real Estate Board. There is, however, another more private form of withdrawal available to him.

The creation of the fairy child whom Babbitt meets in his dreams has often been criticized for its intolerable whimsy. At one level she obviously represents an escape from the oppressive realities of the day:

> Instantly he was in the magic dream. He was somewhere among unknown people who laughed at him. He slipped away, ran down the paths of a midnight garden, and at the gate the fairy child was waiting. Her dear and tranquil hand caressed his cheek. He was gallant and wise and well-beloved; warm ivory were her arms; and beyond perilous moors the brave seas glittered.

While it is certainly true that the language used to describe Babbitt's encounters with the fairy child may be duplicated in *Our Mr. Wrenn* and *Main Street*, here the dissociative impulse and its product are located firmly in Babbitt's unconscious mind. Approaching fifty, worried about smoking too much, strangely discontented with his in many ways enviable lot, Babbitt may seem an admirable metaphor of urban man; but he is fully aware of the passing of time, of youthful dreams not realized, and in one way or the other—by immersing himself in the juvenile tribal rites of his masculine clubs or by cultivating his dream child—he seeks to return to the clear, unambiguous and timeless world of childhood. Indeed, we may postulate an implicit relationship between the fairy child and his younger daughter. Among his family Tinka (the nickname is perhaps deliberately reminiscent of J. M. Barrie's creation) is the one person Babbitt genuinely loves; as yet she is still promises, she has not in Housman's phrase been eaten by the grizzly bear, whereas Verona and Ted as extensions of himself have grievously disappointed. Consequently, the father together with his mirror-image in the shape of his idealized daughter can retreat, freed from the tribulations of the circumstantial, into a fantasy world in order to enact the values denied them by their society. Both the concept and the language in which it is realized are artistically justifiable.

Some commentators have taken exception to the two Babbitts. Frederick J. Hoffman, for example, maintained that there is a parody Babbitt and "a sensitive humane Babbitt, who in his person and in his behaviour cancels the validity and nullifies the success of the other." But we do not have to choose between two versions because no distinction is made between them in the controlling point of view. The persistent strain of the mock-heroic and the hyperbolic in the narrative ensures that we follow the vicissitudes of its hero with interest and amusement but not necessarily with any great involvement. Occasionally, Lewis will introduce a sentence such as the following: "Then round the swimmer, bored by struggling through the perpetual surf of family life, new combers swelled." In this metaphor he detaches

himself from his creation and, simultaneously, evokes some degree of sympathetic response. The most common technique, however, is that of comic
inflation: parking a car becomes a "virile adventure," in order to stop smoking
Babbitt "did everything, in fact, except stop smoking"; his preparations for
leaving the office "were somewhat less elaborate than the plan for a general
European war." The tone of such observations is remarkably consistent and,
paradoxically, in view of the satiric intent they cumulatively serve to create
an affinity between the reader and the comic anti-hero at war with his
inherited world.

One of the fascinations of *Babbitt* is that Lewis's stylistic and conceptual
limitations here become strengths. Georgie or, alternatively, George F. Babbitt, according to the role demanded of him, functions for much of the novel
as an image of ursine amiability familiar only in juvenile literature. The
choice of verbs to illustrate his actions is illuminating. We learn, for instance,
that he "ambled up to Verona's room," "humming and grunting" as he
examines her books; that he roars, rumbles, growls, lumbers, snarls, blun-
ders, and even on occasion squeals and yelps. He snuffs the earth, emits soft
grunts. Indeed, at one point, when confronted by the officials of the Good
Citizens' League, his primitive reaction is not unlike that of Bongo, a bear
in Lewis's pallid little story of that name published in *Cosmopolitan:* "Something black and unfamiliar and ferocious spoke from Babbitt." Of course, a
similar vocabulary is introduced into other novels, most notably in *Elmer
Gantry* and in *Dodsworth,* where Sam and his wife indulge in their bear and
rabbit fantasies; but it is the frequency and consistency of this type of
presentation that one remarks here, even in such happenings as the strange
tribal noises and gestures indulged in by Babbitt and his companions. Taken
in conjunction with the mock-heroic technique, the consequence of this
distinctive point of view is to condition the reader's reaction and awaken a
favourable atavistic response which has the effect of neutralizing Babbitt as
a moral being. He becomes a powerful generic symbol into which ethical
lapses such as hypocrisy and financial chicanery are comfortably absorbed.

Babbitt is a wry, sad and amusing novel with a special tone and unity
unique among Lewis's work. Despite the prompt appropriation of the title
into popular speech, the book, as Lewis wrote to H. L. Mencken, is "not
altogether satire." He added:

> I've tried like hell to keep the boob Babbitt from being merely
> burlesque—hard tho that is at times, when he gets to orating
> before the Boosters' Club lunches. I've tried to make him human
> and individual, not a type.

Like Carol Kennicott Babbitt finally returns to the world he knows best. But he is not quite the same man. Although he seems to transfer his dissociative tendencies to his son and in spite of the fact that he continues in a similar pattern of life, we learn that Babbitt's moral fibre "had been so weakened by rebellion that he was not quite dependable in the more rigorous campaigns of the Good Citizens' League nor quite appreciative of the church." He is not and never will be one of the real villains of Zenith— which, as the radical lawyer Seneca Doane puts it, is a "better place to live in than Manchester or Glasgow or Lyons or Berlin or Turin." The process of apotheosis, which will culminate in the figure of Fred Cornplow, has begun.

V

Dodsworth was Lewis's last novel to be published during the decade and, while the book in some ways reflects his own travel and marital experiences, it continues the exploration of the American character in a traditionally American setting: Europe. The theme obviously recalls James's writings, but the stress on the degradation of the artistic impulse in a mechanized society together with the resolution in terms of the land is oddly reminiscent of Sherwood Anderson.

In seeking to present the story of a human relationship, Lewis by means of his setting complicates and enlarges his subject by examining also an historical and cultural relationship. The Europe of earlier individual fantasies is here offered in a much more circumstantial manner, though it is still, in Jamesian terms, very much the continent seen by the financially privileged outsider. Yet the novel is still the record of an education and attempts to trace, in an admittedly rather unsubtle fashion the growth of an individual consciousness as a result of the frustration between ideas and their translation into action.

Dodsworth has achieved his position as the result of an early and profitable recognition of the concept of functional beauty, that cars "ought to get away from imitating carriages." For him the prospect of designing and manufacturing automobiles is deeply fulfilling: "all the while he dreamed of motors like thunderbolts, as poets less modern than himself might dream of stars and roses and nymphs by a pool." But with the absorption of his company by the U.A.C. his individuality can find no means of expression, and in a new cultural setting the problem is heightened. Like Anderson, Lewis seems to be suggesting that the industrial process depersonalizes and that it erodes the creative talent; fundamental questions of identity of necessity are raised, including that of sexual identity. According to Edith Cortwright, Fran, as a symbol of American womanhood, represents "fear and death," it presumably falls upon her to complete the reeducation of Dodsworth, begun by Nande Azeredo in Paris. But the vicious sentimentality with which his marriage has been suffused survives in the form of guilt.

The dissociation here is from the former self and the way of life that defined it, although the closing words of the novel would suggest that the process can never be complete. *Dodsworth* displays the classic Lewis ambivalences in other ways too, most notably in the stress of the essential decency of Sam and other mid-Westerners such as A. B. Hurd, Matey and her husband Tub Pearson, despite the latter's Pocockian reaction to Paris. At the dinner given by Hurd the dilemma is made explicit as Sam attempts a definition of the nation he and the others have left in terms of the picturesque:

> New York on a winter night, with the theatres blaring and the apartment-houses along Park Avenue vanishing up into the wild sky rosy from a million lights. Vermont on an autumn afternoon, with the maples like torches. Midsummer in Minnesota, where the cornfields talked to themselves, and across miles of rolling wheatland, dimpling to the breeze, you saw the tall red wheat-elevators and the spire of the German Catholic Church. The grave silence of the wilderness: plateaus among the sacred peaks of the Sierra Nevadas, painted buttes in Arizona, Wisconsin lakes caressing in dark waters the golden trunks of Norway pines. The fan-lights above serene old Connecticut doorways in Litchfield and Sharon. Proud cold sunsets in the last five minutes of the Big Game at Thanksgiving-time. . . . Cities of a quarter of a million people with fantastic smoky steel works, like maniac cathedrals, which had arisen in twenty years upon unpeopled sand-barrens. The long road and a rather shaggy, very adventurous family in a squeaky flivver, the new Covered Wagon, starting out to see all the world from Seattle to Tallahassee, stopping to earn their bacon and bread and oil by harvesting; singing at night in tourist camps on the edge of wide-lawned towns.

But these multiple meanings no longer hold; "except for half a dozen homesick souls, each of them admitted that he was going to go on loving, boosting, and admiring America, and remain in Europe as long as he could." The bases of this nostalgia are later transformed when, after experiencing the horrors of New York life, Ross Ireland advances to a receptive Dodsworth the suggestion that the real, the true American now lives abroad. The process of dissociation is seemingly complete.

But Lewis continues to weigh and assess the two types of society. Among the flaws of the novel are the unashamed and lengthy debates of the respective merits of Europe and America. They are oddly reminiscent of the colloquies that Fenimore Cooper with a similar purpose in view inserted into his fiction of the 1830s. Another fault is that the Europe which we are here offered is still very much that of the outsider. Dodsworth may be a latter-day, pragmatic passionate pilgrim but, as he himself realizes, this de luxe Cook's tour of London, Paris, Berlin, Madrid, Rome and Florence isolates him from the other Europe of which he has glimpses only. His involvement with the Sans Souci development therefore becomes an attempt to bridge the Atlantic in personal and architectural terms.

The final choice for America, however, is not made until the closing chapters. It is dependent upon Sam's recognition of the truth of Edith's assertion:

> Here, we may have ruins and painting, but behind them we're
> so much closer to the eternal elements than you Americans. You
> don't love earth, you don't love the wind . . . That's the strength
> of Europe—not its so called "culture," its galleries and neat voices
> and knowledge of languages, but its nearness to earth.

And the weakness of America, correspondingly, is its detachment from the romantic virtues associated with the land. This passage represents a neat inversion of a tradition which goes back to at least the eighteenth century; it may be said to fuse in the values it advances the twin nostalgias for frontier and Europe. Althought the reconstructed Dodsworth promptly begins to dream of an "authentic farm," the final compromise is characteristic of the author: Sam and Edith are to return to the United States to "experiment with caravans," an action that will satisfy his vaguely creative impulses and, at the same time, provide his fellow-countrymen and women with an opportunity to recover that which has been lost from the national life. While admirably democratic, the proposal is hardly the cosmopolitan solution which has been tentatively suggested in earlier pages and it does not acknowledge that the presence of motorized caravans in the wilderness can only succeed in destroying it.

It is an oddly factitious solution expressed in embarrassingly self-conscious prose. Europe, then, is in traditional American fashion tested and rejected in favour of America—though in Lewis's last novel, *World So Wide*, the Dodsworths reappear as permanent expatriates in Florence. Against

Fran's brittle extoleation of European culture Sam can only offer "the tradition of pioneers pushing to the westward, across the Alleghenies, through
the forests of Kentucky and Tennessee, on to the bleeding plains of Kansas,
on to Oregon and California, a religious procession, sleeping always in danger, never resting, and opening a new home for a hundred million people."
In the last months of the decade, however, before the crash of October 1929,
this vision could mean nothing except a sentimental gesture towards the
American past; it is impossible for Lewis—despite such attempts as the
setting up in *Arrowsmith* of reverberations in terms of its opening paragraphs—to translate the virtues of an heroic age into contemporary terms.
He could offer only an increasingly idealized series of portraits of the American middle class until in *The Prodigal Parents* (1938), for the benefit of an
audience to whom his faded iconography meant nothing, he announced the
triumph of the American businessman.

VI

In his essay "Materialism and Idealism in American Life" Santayana
discusses the symbolic American who

> can be made largely adequate to the facts; because if there are
> immense differences between individual Americans—for some
> Americans are black—yet there is a great uniformity in their
> environment, customs, temper, and thoughts. They have all been
> uprooted from their several soils and ancestries and plunged to-
> gether into one vortex, whirling irresistibly in a space otherwise
> quite empty. To be an American is of itself almost a moral con-
> dition, an education, and a career. Hence a single ideal figment
> can cover a large part of what each American is in his character,
> and almost the whole of what most Americans are in their social
> outlook and political judgements.

The source of Lewis's power as a novelist seems to lie in his iconic tran-
scriptions of American life where, it might be argued, the icons are made
largely adequate to the facts. His achievement rests on his ability to identify
the new social dimensions of the vortex and, as a result, his emblematic
fictions examine, albeit obliquely, the implications of the moral condition to
which Santayana alludes. He is America's first distinctively urban as opposed
to city novelist. In *Main Street* he analysed the patterns of a static small-town
community; in *Babbitt* he focussed his attention on the problems of urban
living and in Babbitt produced his single great creation; in *Dodsworth* he may

be said to study by implication some of the consequences of life in a post-industrial society. For Dodsworth, endowed with time and money and released from the functional definition of the self, is able to find in Europe a larger and freer identity than he has known before.

In the 1920s Lewis's sociological fictions made their primary appeal through the satiric observation of phases of contemporary life. Often, however, his novels possessed a special quality that elevated them above the level of mere destructive comment on contemporary folly; this dimension was early recognized by Constance Rourke who pointed out that for all the striking immediacy of his writings Lewis was essentially the fabulist of an older American tradition, a maker of images, who first appropriated and then imaginatively transformed an aspect of national life. He identified and dramatized for his readers certain primary truths concerning the nature of the American character. In so doing he created a fictitious Middle America with its own geography and history and, if he did not develop (at least in his novels) his created region as systematically as Hardy or Faulkner elaborated theirs, in becoming its official mythographer he gave to the world a fable which it welcomed as fact. Even in his best decade the quality of Lewis's work is uneven, illustrating the often remarked ambiguity of his relationship to his material. It is this uncertainty that excludes Lewis's novels from consideration as a primitive pop art, though at times they certainly seem to belong to that category. *Elmer Gantry*, for example, the most pungent and unremitting of all Lewis's castigations of American life, is finally a novel that it is difficult to take seriously. Written with considerable energy and gusto, it contains some of Lewis's wittiest prose; but Elmer himself in the final stages of his progress towards the dictatorship of world morality so conclusively disappears into caricature that he ends as an almost medieval illustration of lechery and hypocrisy incarnate.

The attitudes expressed in the three novels examined here would suggest that of the two types of pastoral impulse discerned by Leo Marx Lewis was closer to the popular variety than to that higher, complex pastoralism that distinguishes much American literature. Indeed, in *Arrowsmith*, an excessively schematized variant on the quest theme, the response produced by the closing pages is one of embarrassment at the simplistic solution and the sentimentality of the prose in which it is expressed. Similarly in both *Main Street* and *Dodsworth* the final resolutions in terms of idealized landscape are uneasy and, ultimately, unconvincing. The resonance that we associate with the genuine work of art is present only in *Babbitt* where Lewis develops the interior landscape of wonder. In these novels the drama is mute; that "capacity for moral heroism" commemorated by nineteenth-century American authors is here reduced to the act of dissociation as the self seeks an identity in and commensurate with urban society. A similar search is reflected in Lewis's own paradigmatic life. The hotel rooms and rented houses of two continents suggest that the most permanent form of dissociation is to be found not in his writings but in Sinclair Lewis himself.

NAN BAUER MAGLIN

Women in Three Sinclair Lewis Novels

Remembering Carol Kennicott's sufferings in her very Middle American marriage in a very Middle American town in the novel *Main Street*, I went back to her story wondering whether her condition still speaks to women today, wondering whether her situation was actually reflective of her day, and wondering whether Sinclair Lewis had written other novels showing a similar sensitivity about the particular circumstances of women in society. By examining two other Lewis novels of lesser fame, *The Job* and *Ann Vickers*, as well as the history and popular culture of the period, I came to the conclusion that, yes, Sinclair Lewis was consciously exploring through fiction the choices and pressures that women felt personally and socially during the first third of the twentieth century. And, yes, this fictional exploration still has relevance emotionally and politically because the choices for and pressures on women have not been significantly modified.

The Job (1917) is about women workers; *Main Street* (1920) explores marriage and motherhood; *Ann Vickers* (1933) depicts both the career woman and the political woman in the suffrage movement. The novels each follow the struggle of a woman—Una Golden, Carol Kennicott, and Ann Vickers— for her identity as a human being. Central to the focus of each novel is the dilemma: work or marriage.

While neither *The Job* nor *Ann Vickers* is of as high a literary quality as *Main Street*, all three novels present acute historical insight into what life was like for women. A comparison of the novels with the social background

From *The Massachusetts Review* 14, no. 4 (Autumn 1973). © 1974 by The Massachusetts Review, Inc.

against which they were written will demonstrate just how well Lewis was reflecting the actualities. The acutal social pressures are especially well seen in the pages of mass media women's magazines—in a sense, they are a barometer of the acceptable role-images for women. The women's magazines played heavily on the themes of marriage and work, varying their tune according to the needs of society and the job market.

During the period of Una Golden's work history in *The Job*, which lasts from 1906 until 1915, magazines oriented towards women conveyed the message that it was all right for women to work but their ultimate goal in life was still marriage and the family. The widely-read *Ladies Home Journal* was especially forthright about propagandizing this theme.

When *Ladies Home Journal* carried articles on women and jobs, especially office jobs, such as "How I Became a Confidential Secretary" (September 1916) and "The Girl Behind the Typewriter: What She Should Do to Earn the Highest Rewards in Work" (May 1915), the attitude that prevailed was that if women had to work, they should at least have jobs which duplicated their roles at home, the boss replacing the husband as the lord and master who must be cheerfully served and encouraged. The *Journal* taught that success on the job meant "self-denial and self-control" and a subjugation of "her own personality in every sense of the word; yet she is not servile." This line of thought was by no means confined to the pages of the *Ladies Home Journal*. Ida Tarbell spells this same theme out very explicitly in the April 1916 *Woman's Home Companion:*

> As things now are I am inclined to think that the most effective training that thousands of girls get for housekeeping is from a period of service in a modern scientifically managed factory, shop or office.

Beyond this, the ultimate message is that work should never be a woman's choice but should only be undertaken out of necessity. The *Ladies Home Journal* of May 1915 carries a short story very neatly designed to convey this idea. A young woman whose father had died and whose brother now supported the family decides to work in an office. She rises very rapidly, apparently because she is exceedingly well groomed and dressed and because she thinks only of business. "She laughed when she pictured herself washing dishes or scrubbing floors, and glanced approvingly at her mirrored self in the trim business get-up." But, alas, she falls ill and while in her sickbed watches her mother endlessly laundering her office outfits. Her mother explains to her that she has gained her freedom at her mother's expense:

You are perhaps better off than you would be at home. You have more broadened interests, more elaborate surroundings, finer clothes, less worry and more rest; in fact you have bettered yourself. But you have deliberately shut your eyes to home interests.

If you had stayed home I should have been relieved of half the work, and, between us, I think we could have contrived to dress you well. I should have had a companion and you would have known the friendship of a mother whose interest is your interest—who would share your sorrow and joy.

But you chose the cold, mechanical, business world, where the interest is only money, and sorrow and joy are devoid of sympathy.

As in this story, women had been given double messages about the virtues of working before and during the War. Once the War was over there was no longer a pressing economic demand for their services; anti-work propaganda was stepped up and work's virtues receded into the background.

In typical doubletalk a 1920 *Ladies Home Journal* article tells us "What the Newest New Woman Is." She is—surprise!—the traditional woman in the home:

Women who are sincerely honest and one-pointed in their desire to rear their children into healthy, intelligent, high-minded maturity come into agreement with old truths. They admit that there is no vocation demanding more mental agility, more subtlety of discretion, more painstaking devotion than the one job of rearing children. They admit that it is a woman-size job, demanding their hours and their minutes.

The article goes on to call women who want to work "self-centered" and unfulfilled:

Every girl who shirks marriage because its homely duties are irksome, every woman who refuses to have children, every mother who needlessly delivers her home and her children into the care of a servant is using her saw-toothed ax on progress. And in selfishly seeking her own comfort or satisfying her personal ambitions, she smothers her womanhood.

While these words may sound almost as if they were lifted from an army recruiting pamphlet, the *Journal*, if anything, laid it on the line even more explicitly in April 1921. Here the woman who puts her working career

before her home is called "a distinct danger to the state, for her path too
often leads away from the home and the child, not toward it."

In all three novels Lewis depicts women who at least in one part of their
lives go to work. In 1906 Una Golden is forced to go to work by economic
necessity; Carol Kennicott holds a job for three years until she marries in
1912; from 1912–1920 Ann Vickers holds a series of different jobs. In all
three cases the work/marriage conflict is excruciating. The choices the three
make regarding career and family reflect more than the progpaganda; they
are also affected by the struggle for women's rights; Carol and Ann even
become activists in the movement for a time.

All three novels are very sensitive to the ebbs and flows of the suffrage
movement. Una begins making her way in the business world when the
movement is in a state of political disarray; Carol and Ann join the movement
in a period when it is in the ascendant. Thus, it is useful to know that
1896–1910 has been called the "doldrums period" in the early women's rights
struggle: women's suffrage referendums were defeated in several states and
none were won; with Susan B. Anthony's death in 1906, the movement
suffered from a lack of unifying leadership; during the early part of the
period racist arguments against the voting power of Blacks and immigrants
were widely used within the suffrage movement as a reason to support votes
for women. In 1910 the movement was somewhat revitalized with the for-
mation of the Congressional Union, later known as the Woman's Party.
From that time until the final adoption of the voting rights amendment to
the U.S. Constitution in 1920, the women's rights movement entered a more
militant and organized stage.

It is against this background that *The Job*, *Main Street*, and *Ann Vickers*
portray the lives of three women.

Until her father dies, Una Golden, heroine of *The Job*, lives the life of
a typical midwestern, middle-class, turn-of-the-century young woman. Since
the family is too poor to send her to college and too respectable to send her
to work, she stays home and helps her mother with the housework. It is her
"unmeditated faith that a woman's business in life was to remain respectable
and to secure a man and consequent security." This "unmeditated faith" was
rather normal for this time as is shown in *Women and Work in America*:

> During the last quarter of the nineteenth century, girls born into
> native white families of some social standing rarely worked out-
> side their homes. By keeping his daughter at school or at home
> a father protected her from the defeminizing influence of the harsh
> world of work, saved her the embarrassment of associating with

men to whom she had not been properly introduced, safeguarded her delicate constitution, and proved to the world that he was capable of providing for all his family's wants. [Robert W. Smuts, *Women and Work in America (Schocken Books, N.Y., 1971)*].

Una is brought up by a mother who is discontented with her marriage and with her life, but not discontented enough to do anything about it. Her mother consciously rejects the feminist movement. "She didn't think it was quite ladylike." When widowed, Una's mother can only weep and waste away for she has no training for wage earning and no sense of herself as an independent person.

Una might have become a copy of her mother. However, upon her father's death in 1904, when she is 24, she is forced to take over the support of herself and her mother. Given this reality, there are only two respectable possibilities for her: teaching or office work. Since it would have been beneath her social position, Una never considers factory work.

Una feels trapped by her limited opportunities and her immediate reaction is to rail at her sex-determined fate: "I *hate* being a woman." She determines to make the best of it, however, and moves to New York City to "become a stenographer, a secretary to a corporation president, a rich woman, free and responsible."

Una typifies a real trend in society. Before 1890 the cities were largely populated by families of poor farmers who had been forced off the land and by poor immigrant families. The young women in these families were forced to go to work by their economic circumstances. Generally, they became servants and factory hands. Middle-class women began to migrate to the cities as the job market began changing. "By 1890 . . . there was a rising demand for women in a variety of white-collar jobs which were free of many of the drawbacks of factory and domestic work. The daughter might take a job, for instance, as salesgirl, clerical worker, telephone operator, or typist. Teaching and nursing were also growing rapidly, and the necessary qualifications for each were well within the reach of the daughters of the lower middle class" [Smuts].

Since women's participation in the work force increased sharply during the Civil War, women workers' numbers continued growing. This was especially the case for office workers in the last years of the nineteenth century. The 1900 census figures show almost 74,000 women employed as bookkeepers, accountants, and cashiers, while over 100,000 were grouped together as stenographers, typists, secretaries, and other so-called white collar jobs. Relative to the total population of 76 million these figures are rather small.

Una, therefore, is still something of a pioneer when she sets out in 1904 to become an office secretary. She goes to secretarial school to learn short-hand, typwriting, grammar, spelling, and letter-composition. She goes from job to job, climbing up a limited career ladder. Towards the beginning of her career, Una is occasionally excited by the romance of big business. But as time goes by Una is more and more weighed down by the exhausting and boring routine of office work. She feels oppressed by the office hierarchy and is discouraged by the lack of opportunity for women in the office.

Lewis describes the women at one of Una's offices as working long and hopelessly over new-fangled time-saving office machines: "machines for opening letters and sealing them, automatic typewriters, dictation phono-graphs, pneumatic chutes." While time-saving, the machines made the jobs even more overspecialized, repetitive, and boring. These turn-of-the-century "Olivetti girls" often break down in despair over the meaninglessness of their jobs and lives:

> Epidemics of hysteria would spring up sometimes, and women of thirty-five or forty—normally well content—would join the old ladies in sobbing. Una would wonder if she would be crying like that at thirty-five—and at sixty-five, with thirty barren, weeping years between.

Three future ends seem open to Una and her sister workers: advance-ment, death, or marriage. Advancement is practically impossible since vir-tually no employer "believed that a woman could bear responsibilities." Most of the women, therefore, were forced to resign themselves to the drudgery of their daily tasks, while some got as far as recognizing that "we *are* exploited, women who are on jobs."

The well-known feminist, Inez Haynes Gilmore, painted an identical picture of the demoralized office worker in a 1912 article for *Harper's Bazaar:*

> She can see clearly the arc of her working career stretching before her: a series of dull, weary years, each exactly like the other, untouched by the impetus of progress and unrewarded by pe-cuniary profit. It is not strange that she becomes utterly languid and uninterested—a human machine going through the mere mo-tions of work.

Nevertheless, some of Una's women friends see the office as paradise compared to the sweatshop of the factory. As one of them, Mamie Magen, says:

if you could ever understand what offices have done for me! On the East Side—always it was work and work and watch all the pretty girls in our block get T.B. in garment-factories, or marry fellows that weren't any good and have a baby every year, and get so thin and worn out; and the garment-workers' strikes and picketing on cold nights. And now I am in an office—all the fellows are dandy and polite—not like the floor superintendent where I worked in a department store; he would call down a cash-girl for making change slow—! I have a chance to do anything a man can do.

Most of the women in the office have never experienced factory or department store work, but they know that Mamie's belief that in the office she would be given a chance to do anything a man could do was "a line of guff." So instead of banking on advancement, these white-collar women see marriage as their passport out of the office grind.

But once a woman becomes a worker, so much stigma is attached to her that finding a mate is difficult. According to many of the men in *The Job*, who seem to echo the media ideologues, working women are vulgar and unfeminine, since "business simply unfits a skirt for marriage." As C. Wright Mills observed, in this period "the office is a production plant for old maids, a modern nunnery." And other novels of this period also portray women in this either/or bind. For example, Booth Tarkington's heroine in *Alice Adams* is caught in an impossible dilemma: to save herself for a respectable and remunerative marriage or to enter the "portal of doom" of the working world—while her family slowly goes down to ruin.

Una decides never to marry and instead to try for advancement. But she changes her mind. She gradually becomes weary of "the airless, unnatural, straining life" of the office, and marries Mr. Schwirtz, a flashy, quick-talking, quick-spending salesman. He refuses to let Una work, even when he is out of a job and they are out of money. Finally, after two joyless and isolated years, Una decides to leave her marriage and return to work.

At the book's conclusion, we see Una transformed. She becomes not only a working woman but a successful one. She forces her company to let her be the first woman in her firm to sell real estate, becomes a sales manager supervising five other women, and finally becomes a partner in a hotel business. Ultimately, all the contradictions for working women so graphically portrayed throughout the novel are melodramatically resolved: Una is a successful businesswoman, a nice boss, and will presently become a wife and mother as well. This pat and rather unrealistic ending tends to invalidate all that goes before. Thus, it is a major problem of the work on the levels of both literary effectiveness and social theory. Atypically, Una finds success on both fronts, home and office.

Throughout the novel, joining the women's struggle never suggests itself as a possibility to Una, perhaps since the movement was concentrating on the vote, only focusing on economic conditions indirectly. In the period covered by the novel, many working women joined the movement anyway, because they saw a connection between the vote and the improvement of women's situation in the economy and in society, but most women did not make this connection. Some of Una's friends do join the feminist movement. But early in her working career when Una is asked whether she would ever go out for suffrage and feminism, she declares, "I don't know anything about them. Most women don't know anything about them—about anything!" Towards the end of the novel, in a period in which the movement is once again prominent on the American scene, she admits to only a distant connection with the movement's ideas of independence and equality for women.

Others of Una's friends turn to the union movement in an attempt to alleviate their sense of hopelessness and helplessness. But Una rejects this path, acting again in the more usual way since, in fact, very little white-collar union organizing of any sort was being done in the pre-First World War era. Thus, while Una is typical in not joining the union and suffrage movements, she is rather atypical in having found such a grand solution to the social contradiction between marriage and work.

Despite this individualistic and nonfeminist solution, the contemporary reviewers called *The Job* a "feminist document" (*The Bookman*); a "true reflection of the career of the workers—not the drones—in the feminist ranks" (*The Dial*); and "an earnest and sincere document in favor of independence and self-expression for women" (*The Nation*). *The Dial* is obviously misstating Una Golden's connection with the feminist movement; she only considers herself, accurately enough, "at least one-third the new independent woman."

Although in *The Job* Sinclair Lewis writes of a woman who succeeds in achieving a type of independence, three years later when he writes *Main Street* he depicts a woman who is wholly trapped into a dependent existence as a wife and mother in a small midwestern town. In a sense, it is Sinclair Lewis's *Diary of a Mad Housewife*. Certainly, the book is an examination of the limitations of life and culture, 1906–1920, in a small town—the aspect of the book on which most critics have tended to concentrate. However, the issue of the stultifying effects of marriage upon women in this era is at least equally prominent and has significance for big cities and small towns alike.

Carol is pictured as a rebellious young woman of the Middle West. She has no ties, having lost her parents as a child. First she goes to Blodgett College and then to library school in Chicago. She is a restless woman, interested in causes and clubs. She consciously rejects a life of housekeeping and dishwashing because she wants to be active in the world and not se-questered in the home.

Rather abruptly, after three years of working as a librarian in St. Paul, Carol marries Dr. Will Kennicott of Gopher Prairie. She marries him because "she is slightly weary of her employment and sees no glory ahead." She does see glory ahead in an alliance with a doctor; as the wife of a doctor, she can dedicate herself to uplifting the town. In addition, Dr. Kennicott, who is twelve years older than Carol, provides her with "a shelter from the per-plexing world."

The rest of the novel details Carol's disillusionment with marriage and its jobs: housekeeper, husband-tender, childbearer. This disillusionment be-gins the moment she arrives in Gopher Prairie, her new home. She suddenly feels Will Kennicott to be a stranger to her and a distasteful one at that. She realizes he is coarse, drab, and unimaginative. However, she is not ready to heed her momentary intuition that in order to preserve her sanity and her identity "she would have to wrench loose from this man and flee." Worse than her repulsion for her husband is her realization that the myths of marriage are only myths:

> Why do these stories lie so? They always make the bride's home-coming a bower of roses. Complete trust in noble spouse. Lies about marriage. I'm *not* changed. And this town—O my God! I can't go through with it. This junk-heap!

She is disappointed to learn that she is still Carol Kennicott; marriage has caused no magical transformation.

After this first traumatic day, with Will "escaped to the world of men's affairs," Carol tries to adjust herself to her new life. She tries to take pride in being a housewife. Nevertheless, depite her real efforts to be happy in her new role, she can see herself only as a servant and her home as a prison. Significantly, Carol Kennicott's life in *Main Street* struck a chord of recog-nition in many women. Sinclair Lewis received numerous letters from women who saw Carol's prison as their own.

Nevertheless Lewis appears to understand that, given the limited al-ternatives open to women in that era, many women viewed marriage as a blessed haven. Vida Sherwin, for one, at thirty-nine, after years of teaching school, is literally esctatic over her own wedding. She "was hungry for housework, for the most pottering detail of it. She had no maid, nor wanted one. She cooked, baked, swept, washed supper-cloths, with the triumph of a chemist in a new laboratory. To her the hearth was veritably the altar."

Carol, though, sees very limited alternatives for herself: "have children; start her career of reforming; or become so definitely a part of the town that she would be fulfilled by the activities of church and study-club and bridge parties." A fourth option, employment, is taboo for a married woman, especially a doctor's wife in a small town. Carol tries all three of the options which are open to her.

She first fears and postpones pregnancy, seeing a baby, quite realistically, as the final lock on her prison. Yet she desires something to commit herself to. And so she has a baby. Hugh, her son, becomes simultaneously her reason for living and her jailer. Carol also works frenetically "reforming" the town and organizing women's clubs. But finding none of these activities satisfying, in desperation, she finally goes beyond the accepted alternatives for respectable married women. She begins but never consummates an affair. In the end, a combination of fear and the realization that another man is not her answer serve to restrain her.

She demands and wins a room of her own from a wounded and uncomprehending husband. Like the heroines of Kate Chopin's *The Awakening* and Doris Lessing's "To Room Nineteen," Carol tries to close the door on the demands of the world.

Carol is growing emotionally more desperate as the novel progresses. She swings between the extremes of love and hate toward her husband and home; she rebukes herself for her feelings of dissatisfaction; she feels isolated and friendless; she reverts to childlike behavior and girllike fears; she longs for a father-protector; she rages; she is immobilized; she dreams of escape; she succumbs to the ghostlike performance of her routines. She edges close to hysteria and insanity. At thirty she begins to fantasize about killing people with carving knives. She thrashes around for something or someone to flee to —a room, a male, her fantasies. She has sleepless nights envisioning Will first married to another woman, then imprisoned, then dead. She goes deeper and deeper into a depressed and desperate state.

If *The Job* describes the emotional frustration of the working woman, *Main Street* details the same condition in the middle-class housewife. Like those of the 1950s described by Betty Friedan in *The Feminine Mystique*, the middle-class housewife of the years around World War I faced an overabundance of spare time, feelings of inadequacy, boredom, and uselessness. In the November 1921 *Ladies Home Journal*, Dr. Abraham Meyerson describes the symptoms of this "disease" to be hidden or open dissatisfaction, discontent, and disgust. He correctly locates the cause of "the neurosis of the housewife" as having "a large part of its origin in the increasing desires of women, in their demands for a fuller, more varied life than that afforded by the lot of the housewife." The solution Meyerson offers to women is fairly typical of the inadequate and superficial advice dispensed by the mass media of this period: the "neurotic housewife" should take a rest or a vacation or join a club. Her husband should show her more love and sympathy. If all else fails, Meyerson suggests separation—but not divorce. The media virtually admitted that there was no real solution within accepted modes of behavior for women in Carol Kennicott's predicament.

It is interesting to note that many feminist leaders of the period, such as Inez Haynes Gilmore, Jane Addams, Charlotte Perkins Gilman, and Margaret Sanger, describe themselves in their autobiographies as having gone through the "nervous housewife" stage. As part of their own solutions to the problem of finding an unconfined way of living their lives, many prominent feminists broke up their marriages. Carol Kennicott finally takes this road, also, and does what she suspected from the beginning would be necessary by "stalking out of the Doll's House." She declares to her flabbergasted husband:

> But was I more happy when I was drudging? [before she got her maid] I was not. I was just bedraggled and unhappy. It's work— but not my work. I could run an office or a library, or nurse and teach children. But solitary dish-washing isn't enough to satisfy me—or many other women. We're going to chuck it. We're going to wash 'em by machinery, and come out and play with you men in the offices and clubs and politics you've cleverly kept for yourselves! Oh, we're hopeless, we dissatisfied women! Then why do you want to have us about the place, to fret you? So it's for your sake that I'm going.

It should be noted that many feminists of this period were urging that technological developments and labor-saving devices be employed to free women from housework.

Carol takes her son and moves to Washington, D.C., working for the Bureau of War Risk Insurance. She finds a "home, her own place and her own people" among militant suffragists who "when they were not being mobbed or arrested, took dancing lessons or went picnicking up the Chesapeake Canal or talked about the politics of the American Federation of Labor."

After one year passes, Will Kennicott visits Carol. Although he wants her to return to Gopher Prairie, he does not pressure her. Carol, somewhat confused, consults the "generalissima of suffrage" as to her predicament. The suffrage leader says she is giving Carol the advice she would give to any woman who came to her:

> I'm thinking of thousands of women who come to Washington
> and New York and Chicago every year, dissatisfied at home and
> seeking a sign in the heavens—women of all sorts, from timid
> mothers of fifty in cotton gloves, to girls just out of Vassar who
> organize strikes in their own father's factories!

She tells Carol that if she is not willing to give up everything, including her son, she should return home and work for feminism there. She says:

> you can keep on looking at one thing after another in your home
> and church and bank, and ask why it is, and who first laid down
> the law that it had to be that way.

It is unclear whether Sinclair Lewis is reflecting or merely mocking conditions in the feminist movement. The advice the "generalissima" gives is obviously unrealistic for Carol (though politically the movement needs extension). She tells Carol to go back home, back to the original source of her oppression, and be a radical in isolation from the movement—unless she is willing to give up her son, even though she has been doing well enough with him for over a year.

So, Carol returns to Gopher Prairie, Main Street, and her husband. She is pregnant with a second child and, at first, pregnant with commitment to bring feminism to the hinterland. Her baby girl is born and her commitment slowly dies as the demands of the storm-windows, the hunting trip, and all the petty details of life on Main Street take precedence.

In large measure, the differences between Carol Kennicott in *Main Street* and Una Golden in *The Job* stem from their economic circumstances. Una was compelled to work, but Carol, apparently, was not. Una had a high school education, whereas Carol had a graduate school education. Una's marriage was totally unsuccessful in the conventional sense that her husband was unemployed, penniless, and a drinker, whereas Carol's marriage was eminently successful by all the conventional criteria. Moreover, Una had no children when she left her marriage, but Carol did. And Una operated in an urban environment where there were at least some opportunities for employment and independence; small town life provided Carol with none of this.

Although it might seem that in some ways Carol had more in her favor than Una, one other factor enters the picture. *The Job* was written in 1917 when the war was creating a need for women workers. By 1920, when *Main Street* saw print, the war was over and women were being shooed back into the home to warm the hearth. To some extent, then, finding a resolution to the novel in independence, however limited, might have seemed less likely to Lewis in 1920 than it had been three years before.

In *Ann Vickers* (1933), Lewis retraces his way through the same time period that he covered in *The Job* and in *Main Street*, again dealing with the same general theme of a woman struggling to find a meaningful way of living her life. And then he continues by tracing Ann Vickers's subsequent history through the 1920s. Ann attempts to define herself in terms of work like Una Golden; she tries to find a way of viably relating to the home and family like Carol Kennicott; and—in a fuller way than Carol did—she experiments with living the life of a radical and a feminist.

Ann's wide range of interests and experience should be considered representative of a whole generation of human experience, a whole period of social history. Viewed in this way, the kaleidoscopic events and seemingly superficial character portrayal become comprehensible.

So, at the turn of the century, Ann Vickers of Waubanakee, Illinois is at age ten already a budding socialist and feminist. Oscar Klebs, a German cobbler, teaches her about socialism while her own experiences teach her an elementary kind of feminism. She realizes that "except in the arts of baseball and spitting, she knew herself as good a man" as her male playmates. Understanding that it is a man's world and feeling that she can never compete in terms of traditional femininity, she makes up her mind that she really only has one choice:

> The boys, the ones I want, they'll never like me. And golly, I
> do like them! But I just got to be satisfied with being a boy
> myself.

While ten might be a rather precocious age to be making such momentous decisions, the feminist Inez Haynes Irwin, writing in *The Nation*, recalls a parallel development in her own life:

> Like all young things I yearned for romance and adventure. It
> was not however, a girl's kind of romance and adventure that I
> wanted, but a man's. I wanted to run away to sea, to take tramping
> trips across the country, to go on voyages of discovery and ex-
> ploration, to try my hand at a dozen different trades and occu-
> pations. I wanted to be a sailor, a soldier. I wanted to go to prize
> fights; to frequent barrooms; even barber shops and smoking

rooms seemed to offer a brisk, salty taste of life. I could not have
been more than fourteen when I realized that the monotony and
the soullessness of the lives of the women I knew absolutely
appalled me.

Ann's critical-mindedness regarding sexual roles continues through college. While in college she organizes a socialist club. She begins to do things
no "proper lady" would do. After graduation from 1912 until 1916 she
becomes a full-time activist for the suffrage movement. At 23, Ann and four
other women are sent as a team of organizers to Clateburn, Ohio which is
depicted as a major organizing center for the national suffrage movement.
Actually, between 1906 and 1913 when the National American Woman's
Suffrage Association had no formal headquarters, the small city of Warren,
Ohio—for which Clateburn appears to be the analogue—was considered the
informal headquarters.

Organizing in a small midwestern town and the surrounding region was
not easy. Housewives, especially, tended to be hostile, making such depre-
catory comments as, if "you had to *work* like me, you wouldn't have no time
to think about the vote, no more'n I do! "Nevertheless they succeeded,
despite the harassment of police and male hecklers, in holding several large
meetings. But Ann eventually became fed up with the routine of the suffrage
movement which seemed to be going nowhere. She tires not only of the
tedium of addressing envelopes,

> but of the whole theological vocabulary of suffrage: "economic
> independence of women," "equal rights," "equal pay for equal
> work," "matriarchy." Like such senile words as "idealism," "vir-
> tue," "patriotism," they had ceased to mean anything. And she
> was tired too of the perpetual stories about women's wrongs.
> There were plenty of wrongs, Heaven knew: young widows with
> three children working twelve hours a day for just enough to
> starve slowly on; intelligent women ridiculed and made small by
> boisterous husbands. But the women who came to tea at the
> Fanning Mansion merely to say that their husbands did not ap-
> preciate their finer natures, to them Ann had listened long
> enough.

Despite the fact that Ann leaves the suffrage movement, the novel does
present (as *Main Street* and *The Job* did not) the possibility of women living
and working together as an alternative to or, at least, a support against the
traditional tracks for women. Further, the problems and possibilities of

emotional (and even sexual) intimacy between women is tentatively explored, making the sisterhood of the women's movement seem more real in this novel than it does in *Main Street*.

After leaving the suffrage movement, Ann retains her social commitment. The novel follows her career from her settlement house work, to dispense of money for a female philanthropist, to her officership of the Organized Charities Institute, to her educational directorship of Green Valley Refuge for Women, to prison reformer. She gets her Ph.D., writes books, and does public speaking. Ultimately, she is a "successful" woman within the rules of the system—a sort of Una Golden enlarged.

During the 1920s Ann becomes more moderate, gradually replacing her earlier radical views with liberal ones. Lewis is portraying the effects of an era which saw the receding of the pre-war radical wave. There was no mass women's movement. The only significant women's struggle was the Woman's Party fight for the Equal Rights Amendment in the early part of the decade. The period was dominated by the growth of conservatism when "the liberalism of the Progressive era was replaced by the hysteria of the Red Scare." Lewis depicts Ann's political development as the mirror image of the era.

The novel also traces the unfolding of her personal and emotional life. She sleeps with a solider, gets pregnant, and has an abortion. She marries at 40 and finds herself in a similar situation to Carol Kennicott in that she tries to be a good wife to a loving but very dull businessman. But her situation differs sharply from Carol's in that Ann is by this time a successful individual whose success is seen as a threat by her husband. She separates from her husband and begins an affair with Judge Barney Dolphin, a married man who soon becomes indicted in a bribery scandal. She bears Barney's baby while he goes to prison for four years. When Barney finally gets out, they begin a life together. At the novel's end, she feels free and complete. In Sinclair Lewis's inadvertently amusing wrap-up, Ann is:

> the Captive Woman, the Free Woman, the Great Woman, the
> Feminist Woman, the Domestic Woman, the Passionate Woman,
> the Cosmopolitan Woman, the Village Woman—the Woman.

In all three novels—*The Job*, *Main Street*, and *Ann Vickers*—Lewis is grappling with the problem of how women are to find meaningful lives within American society. Despite the fact that Lewis was pro-radical and pro-feminist, he wrote in a 1929 article for *The Pictorial Review* that women should strive for individual rather than collective success:

> No, I do not present America as desirable for women because it
> gives them an easy life, but precisely because it gives them a hard

life—a keen, belligerent, striving, exciting life of camp and em-
battled field; because it gives them a part in the revolution which
. . . is changing all our world from the lilac-hedged cottages of
Main Street to the overpowering, the intimidating, yet magnifi-
cent bastions of Park Avenue.

Women not only can take full part in this revolution—they are
taking it, and such women, though they may long to return to
the lilacs and roses and peace of Main Street, are certainly not
returning. If they can not utterly enjoy being warriors, they can
never now enjoy anthing less valiant.

But these celebrated ladies [politicians, businesswomen, writers, actresses, religous leaders, etc.] I bring in only as a hint that,
increasingly, the greatest careers in this country are open to
women. But that fact, applying only to a few women of extraordinary vigor, or charm, or intelligence, or instinct for publicity,
is less important than the fact that everywhere in America women
have, if they care to seize it, a power and significance at least
equal to that of men about them.

Thus, the success-story endings of *The Job* and *Ann Vickers* which seem
so contrived were not thought of in this light by Lewis. He believed such
successes to be quite possible and evidently intended these two novels both
to portray the reality of this type of success and to serve as an inspirational
piece to spur women on to emulate his heroines, Una Golden and Ann
Vickers. In *Main Street*, he is showing us the other side—what happens when
success is not achieved and the fight for it is given up.

It is wrong, I think, to dwell on the conclusions of each of Lewis's three
novels, however. The real value of these works lies in the fact that he views
life for women in American society as a struggle against very oppressive and
very stubborn obstacles. Beyond this, *The Job*, *Main Street*, and *Ann Vickers*
are historical documents which preserve for us the struggles of women in
our past to solve some of the very same problems that still exist in society
today.

MARTIN LIGHT

Dodsworth: The Quixotic Hero

Dodsworth resolves a tension that has resided within Lewis's romantic
heroes from the beginning of her career—the tension childishly expressed
by Milt Daggett in *Free Air:* "Wonder if a fellow could be a big engineer,
you know, build bridges and so on, and still talk about, oh, beautiful things?"
For Samuel Dodsworth is another quixotic hero who has taken most of his
ideas from romantic novels and booster oratory, who sets out on travels of
adventure, and who transforms what he sees by using his fanciful imagination. By the end of the novel, however, Sam will be ready to dismiss
much of his quixotism. This action is symbolized principally by his separation from his wife (who herself is a figure of romantic yearnings); but
additionally we see it in such a moment as when Edith Cortright (whom
Sam has now courted rightly, with common sense and clear vision) influences
Sam's designs for a housing development he intends to supervise in Zenith
in his new career. Sam's "San Souci Gardens" are to consist of imitative
houses—"Italian villas and Spanish patios and Tyrolean inns and Tudor
manor-houses and Dutch Colonial farmhouses." But Edith advises him otherwise: "Sam! About your suburbs. Something could be done—not just Italian
villas and Swiss chalets. . . . Why shouldn't one help to create an authentic
and unique American domestic architecture? . . . Create something native. . . . Dismiss the imitation châteaux."

We can sigh with relief. No more châteaux of the kind we have had for
Wrenn, Istra, Hawk, Ruth, Milt, Claire, Carol Kennicott, Guy Pollock, and

From *The Quixotic Vision of Sinclair Lewis.* © 1975 by the Purdue Research Foundation,
West Lafayette, Indiana. Purdue University Press, 1975.

Arrowsmith, as well as for Sam. In this novel both Lewis and his protagonist seem to be working their way free of quixotism. However, we have only to wait for the next novel to see Lewis's old yearnings return.

Dodsworth opens with the language of romance. In a prelude to the story proper, Sam is attending a dance, in a setting called "a sentimental chromo." Young Samuel Dodsworth, like other Lewis heroes before him, sees his idealized girl come to life. He knows at once that "after years of puzzled wonder about the purpose of life, he had found it." It is Fran Voelker, "slim, shining, ash-blonde, her self-possessed voice very cool as she parried the complimentary teasing of half a dozen admirers." Sam is entranced by the sight of Fran. He searches his romantic mind for metaphors for her. He sees himself as a Richard Harding Davis hero; he is "riding a mountain trail, two thousand sheer feet above a steaming valley; sun-helmet and whipcord breeches; tropical rain on a tin-roofed shack." Fran declares that she is grasping; she wants the whole world. Sam promises it to her. She seems a reincarnation of Carol Kennicott, and the connection is established by Fran's "too-gorgeous lounging robe of Chinese brocade," like the costume of the Princess Winky Poo of *Main Street*. Sam's angel is "an angel of ice."

After this prelude the novel skips twenty years of marriage, during which Sam was too busy with his work to be discontented. The story picks up at the point of Sam's retirement from business. He is fifty; Fran is forty-one; the year is 1925. Sam awakens to doubts about his angel; she is too much a manager, she plays at being a kitten, but "she's a greyhound." "She's quicksilver. And quicksilver is hard, when you try to compress it!" Soon enough we are told what Fran can do to her husband: "She had a high art of deflating him, of enfeebling him with one quick, innocent-sounding phrase. . . . The easy self-confidence which weeks of industrial triumphs had built up in him she could flatten in five seconds. She was, in fact, a genius at planting in him an assurance of his inferiority."

Fran persuades Sam to tour Europe. After twenty years of marriage and with their children grown up, she desires a "new life" before it's too late; she wants to be free. Quickly they sail. And quickly we learn what her new life is to mean: aboard ship "within three days she had a dozen men to 'play with.'" Again, Lewis indicates that he no longer admires the young yearner who wishes to play; it is now his Managers and Improvers who play.

Sam's quixotism is fed by books and by travel pictures, which utter magic names; St. Moritz, Cannes, the Grand Canal. He recalls the romanticizing of earlier days, when he would come to the nursery of his daughter Emily and say, "Milord, the Duke of Buckin'um lies wownded [sic] at the gate!" As he and Fran approach Europe he calls forth the inspiration of his wanderlust, Kipling, from whose "The Gipsy Trail" he recites "Follow the Romany patteran."

As the ship nears Britain, Sam feels that "they had fulfilled the adventure, . . . they had come home to England." His imagination is released; he sees and he fancies. We note the images from books that shaped his vision:

> Mother England! Land of his ancestors; land of the only kings who, to an American schoolboy, had been genuine monarchs— Charles I and Henry VIII and Victoria. . . . Land where still, for the never quite matured Sammy Dodsworth, Coeur de Lion went riding, the Noir Faineant went riding, to rescue Ivanhoe, where Oliver Twist still crept through evil alleys, where Falstaff's belly-laugh discommoded the godly, where Uncle Ponderevo puffed and mixed, where Jude wavered by dusk across the moorland, where Old Jolyon sat with quiet eyes, in immortality more enduring than human life.

Lewis declares, "Just like in the pictures! England!" Sam's fancy carries him further: "Knights in tourney; Elaine in white samite, mystic, wonderful— no, it was Guinevere who wore the white samite, wasn't it? must read some Tennyson again. Dukes riding out to the Crusades with minstrels playing on—what was it?—rebecks? Banners alive." But, he reflects, "it isn't real! It's fiction! the whole thing, village and people and everything, is an English novel—and I'm in it!"

As with other quixotes, Sam perceives in two steps. First he fancies an image or a story of the object he is confronting; then he is shaken back to reality. For example, we are told that Sam "discovered slowly, and always with a little astonishment, that the French were human." He asks himself, "Just what did I expect in France? Oh, I don't know. Funny! . . . Guess I thought there wouldn't be any comforts—no bathrooms, and everybody taking red wine and snails for breakfast, . . . and all the men wearing waxed mustaches and funny beards." We are reminded of Carol Kennicott's fantasy of a romantic Frenchman. Sam thinks he should hear Frenchmen say, "Ze hired girl iz vun lovely girl—oo la la—." But of course they say nothing of the kind, and for putting such clichés in his mind, Sam thanks two sources: "They lie so! These speakers at club meetings, and these writers in the magazines!"

The confrontation with reality occurs when he first stereotypes the journalist called Ross Ireland, whom Sam thinks will be shallow-minded, before he comes to understand the "truth" about him: "Sam discovered that Ross Ireland was guilty of reading vast and gloomy volumes of history; that he admired Conrad more than Conan Doyle." This is the Sweeney Fishberg effect, the Oxford Chinese effect. Again, when Sam attends a college reunion he sees Don Binder, "in college a generous drinker, baby-faced and milky, now an Episcopalian rector." Another former classmate was now a major general, "and one—in college the most mouselike of bookworms—was the funniest comedian on Broadway." Once more we hear of the stereotype: "The great traveler of the novelists is tall and hawk-nosed, speaking nine languages, annoying all right-thinking persons by constantly showing drawing-room manners. He has 'been everywhere and done everything.' He has shot lions in Siberia and gophers in Minnesota, and played tennis with the King at Stockholm." But the *real* traveller is actually "a small mussy person in a faded green fuzzy hat, inconspicuous in a corner of the steamer bar." Thus when Sam encounters anyone new, he creates a picture and story of that person, later to be corrected. When he first sees Edith Cortright, who will subsequently be his wife, he thinks: "She's definitely a 'great lady.' Yet I'll bet that at heart she's lonely." We hear echoes of William Wrenn, from the first novel. Soon Edith declares, "I really love housekeeping. I should have stayed in Michigan and married a small-town lawyer." She might be a reformed and contented Carol Kennicott. Sam and Edith see Naples as Carol's vision made real: "The villas along the bay were white and imposing upon the cliff-tops, at the head of sloping canyons filled with vines and mulberries, or, set lower, mediaeval palaces of arcaded and yellowed marble with their foundations in the water."

As Sam views Europe, listens to talk, and thinks, he seems to develop. He plans a change: "He would have a second life; having been Samuel Dodsworth he would go on and miraculously be some one else, more ruthless, less bound, less sentimental. He could be a poet, a governor, an explorer." "He was so tired of dragging out his little soul and worrying over it!"

Dodsworth has been sorely troubled. He knows that his dissatisfaction with America is also a deep dissatisfaction with himself. He asks himself why he had ever gone abroad. "It had unsettled him. . . . How was it that this America, which had been so surely and comfortably in his hand, had slipped away?" Not since *Main Street* and *Babbitt* has a character in Lewis's fiction been so deeply disturbed, so torn among values, so ready for that conflict of person and society which can result in character growth and change.

Lewis believes that such an inner dissatisfaction is not typically European but is peculiarly American. In his crisis Dodsworth, having abandoned business as the foundation of his philosophy, has nothing to put in its place. Religion means nothing to him ("I'd give my left leg if I could believe what the preachers say. Immortality. Serving Jehovah. But I can't. Got to face it alone.") He has a naive and romantic sense of history—upon his reading that the site of Notre Dame was earlier occupied by a temple of Jupiter, he thinks: "temple of Jupiter. Priests in white robes. Sacrificial bulls with patient wondering eyes, tossing their thick garlanded heads. Chariots . . . The past . . . was suddenly authentic." By being cut off from tradition, he is truly innocent and new, and he must find all things for himself once again. America provides but one cluster of immediate and dramatic definitions of life—success, wealth, and position. It offers no opportunity—no real freedom—for its young people to question the pursuit of happiness and to choose among alternatives.

We should not forget that Fran Dodsworth has her own perception of the defects of America and her own flirtation with European values. She believes that American men do not *like* women enough. They do not provide an ideal worthy of women's sacrifice; certainly the manufacture of motorcars is no ideal. Fran is everywhere entranced by lords and countesses, stately homes, and refined manners. She is drawn into affairs with two examples of European corruption: Arnold Israel, who though an American is in the European—or, as Fran says, "oriental"—tradition of seducers, and Kurt von Obersdorf, who, it turns out, betrays Fran because of subservience to his mother. When the break with Fran comes, Dodsworth celebrates the event with that strange Parisian exotic named Nande Azeredo, who is surely one of Lewis's most striking compounds of fanciful traits. In her, both Lewis and by extension Dodsworth indulge their powers of quixotic enchantment.

Nande has an important role to play in *Dodsworth*, for Sam, the heretofore monogamous hero, spends three days and nights with her as a gesture of his estrangement from his wife. Lewis does not want to provide Dodsworth with a good woman who would divert attention from the crucial affair with Edith Cortright which is yet to come, for the later love is to be mature, platonic, and deep in mutural understanding. Nor can Sam go to a prostitute for one night. So Lewis creates Nande Azeredo. She is a bohemian, an individualist, an amoralist with her own kind of loyal morality. She is described as "a tall, rather handsome girl, with a face as broad between the check bones as a Tartar." Approaching Sam, she demands "in an English that sounded as though it were played on a flute, 'Vot's the trouble? You look down in the mout.' " Now follow details that stamp the fantastic upon this portrait of Nande: she is "half Portuguese, half Russian, and altogether French." Numbers mean a lot in building her characterization. At twenty-five, "she had lived in nine countries, been married three times, and once shot a Siberian wolf." Is this not enough? The joke must broaden, even at the cost of stifling the reader's credulity. More exoticism follows: "She had been a chorus girl, a dress mannequin, a masseuse, and now she scratched out a thin living by making wax models for show-window dummies and called herself a sculptress. She boasted that though she had had fifty-seven lovers ('And, my dear, one was a real Prince—well, pretty real'), she had never let one of them give her anything save a few frocks." Along with her exoticism and goodness of heart, Nande knows how to "serve her man," assuring him "that he was large and powerful and real." The result is that "for the first time in his life [Dodsworth] began to learn that he need not be ashamed of the body which God had presumably given him but which Fran had considered rather an error."

Here in her dishevelled flat, amidst dolls, clothes in heaps, and seven canaries, Nande appears to have run away with Sam's good sense and with Lewis's as well. Sam and Lewis together plunge into every fantasy in the repertoire: "What a wife she'd make for a pioneer! She'd chuck this Parisian show like a shot, if she loved somebody. She'd hoe the corn, she'd shoot the Indians, she'd nurse the babies—and if she couldn't get Paris lingerie, she'd probably spin it." Nande could stand as a fabulous figure, but the difficulty is that here she is required for a serious purpose. Lewis wishes the episode to show Sam at a moment of growth in understanding. Instead, we have an author's dream interlude which in another context would be a joke but here distracts from a critical moment in Sam's development.

The last chapters of *Dodsworth* contain, nevertheless, some of the best non-satiric passages Lewis ever wrote—and his best conclusion of a novel. If we are by now prepared to grant Lewis his defects, which seem inevitable, we can see that in *Dodsworth* he keeps them subdued and exploits his strengths. He controls the tone almost completely. He makes clear what Dodsworth is learning from his new companion, Edith Cortright. If the answers to the search are, after all, fairly obvious, they are convincing under the circumstances. The values are embodied in art, in repose, in building and creating, in good talk, and most of all in a sound relationship between persons.

Two passages momentarily disturb the tone. In an ugly phrase he has Edith say something out of keeping with her generous nature: in rejecting New York, she tells Sam that "Russian Jews in London clothes going to Italian restaurants with Greek waiters and African music"—mongrels, she calls them—have contaminated it. In the other passage, we learn that, true to popular fiction and soap operas, the widow Edith Cortright has had an unhappy first marriage. Her late husband was a liar, a drunkard, a brute. Lewis thus gave his hero and lady an occasion for some sentimental sobbing.

But he missed the opportunity to dignify Edith by providing her with a mature experience in a happy first marriage.

Nevertheless, all else is well controlled. We are led by a series of comparisons with Fran to understand what Edith stands for: Edith is easy and gay, finds everything in life amusing, keeps her hair long and parted simply "in an age of universal bobbing." Most of all (here we are in the midst of complex attitudes where Lewis is searching once again for just the right balance) she regards painting as neither superior nor inferior to manufacturing (Fran thought it superior): "I neither regard it as inferior, as do your Chambers of Commerce who think that all artists are useless unless they're doing pictures for stocking advertisements, nor do I regard it as superior, as do all the supercilious lady yearners who suppose that a business man with clean nails prefers golf to Beethoven." Sam agrees. His own conclusion is that modern businessmen are "about like other people, as assorted as cobblers, labor leaders, Javanese dancers, throat specialists, whalers, minor canons, or asparagus-growers."

Sams finds in Edith sympathy and respect. She is a good cook, she loves housekeeping, swimming, sailing, tennis. In Europe, she says, one can have dignity and privacy. Together they have long, slow, peaceful talks. Sam feels as if he is beginning to change.

So rare is it for Lewis to juxtapose emotions that it is a pleasant surprise to regard the skill with which he cuts across Sam's awakening contentment by means of Fran's shrill-voiced letters. Fran had just written him a long letter ending with shock at the familiarity between her lover the count and his servants; Sam at once thinks of Edith and her kind way with employees. We are told that "in the twilight hush, Edith's voice was quiet, not pricking him with demands for admiration of her cleverness, her singular charms, but assuring him . . . that she was happy to be with him."

In keeping with his ideas about the strength of the pioneers and the influence of the west wind, Lewis gives Edith a speech in which she reveals the message of Europe, the cause of America's failing, and her formula for regeneration through primitivism. Often she lies in her garden, under the hot sun, smelling the earth, finding life. Sam responds as she advises; "he turned to the eternal earth, and in the earth he found contentment."

More letters from Fran intrude, in which Dodsworth reads that Fran has been betrayed by her lover. Lewis handles plot and character admirably here. True to his nature, Sam loyally leaves Edith in order to help Fran; true to her nature, Fran is the same, as self-centered and nagging as ever. In a climax in which Sam's growth and change are proved, he returns to Edith, convincingly saddened about his wife, but equally certain that reunion with her would mean little to her and death to his spirit. *Dodsworth* is Lewis's tribute to Europe's values and to America's energy and capacity to learn. So ends the dialectic in Lewis's books. He has evolved a way to fuse, in one man, the thinker and the builder, the sensitive artist and the pragmatic realist. From this point Lewis must seek new attitudes, new perceptions of life, or forever repeat himself. Unfortunately, repetition is what followed.

The problem of investing the eternal doers (as he called Dodsworth and Myron Weagle and Fred Cornplow) with believeable heroic qualities was difficult to solve. The rebels and the pariahs like Guy Pollock and Miles Bjornstam of *Main Street* were destined to fail; they do not fail nobly, but pathetically, for Lewis made them weak and intended them to be subordinate to the major figures. Arrowsmith and Dodsworth, however, have some measure of intelligence and dignity, though both have deficiencies as heroes. But some of these deficiencies were intended to indicate that typically American heroes "bumble" and "clump" as well as stride. Whatever Lewis wished to leave to the world as the message of the doers, he left best in *Dodsworth* rather than in any other book.

Professor Grebstein observes that "the critics who have complained that Lewis was incapable of anything but mockery, those who have asserted that Lewis's characters are flat or grotesque, those who deny Lewis any stature beyond that of historian of part of the mood of the 1920's could not have read *Dodsworth*." The book is, in fact, one of Lewis's highest achievements.

His almost indiscriminate ambivalence of attitude toward his characters is shown in his late diary entries. At sixty-one years of age he was still perplexed about those American men whom he had tried to portray during the previous thirty years. He had just spent a long afternoon with "the boys" on a motor-cruiser exploring the Duluth-Superior Harbor. He had been in company with an insurance broker, two bankers, and four real-estate men. They were kindly, touching, lonely. They did charitable work; they told jokes; they belonged to church; they hated Roosevelt and cooperatives. They were kind to an outsider.

These garrulous tellers of dirty stories, these men just marginally honest, these merchants of Zenith—they did the world's building, they could be such good, unselfish fellows. He scorned them, but he *liked* them. Therefore, late in life, Lewis created a new and fond name for them—they were his "Babbittworths."

Chronology

1885	Harry Sinclair Lewis born February 7 at Sauk Centre, Minnesota, second son of Edwin J. Lewis and Emma Kermott Lewis.
1891	Lewis's mother dies.
1890–92	Attends public schools in Sauk Centre. Father remarries Isabel Warnper in 1892.
1901–3	Writes and works as a typesetter for Sauk Centre *Herald* and Sauk Centre *Avalanche*. Attends school at Oberlin Academy in preparation for Yale.
1903–6	Attends Yale. Writes for Yale *Literary Magazine* and *Courant*; edits *Literary Magazine*. Travels to England during the summers of 1904 and 1906. Returns to Sauk Centre in 1905 and plans the novel *The Village Virus*.
1906	Leaves Yale. Lives on Upton Sinclair's utopian farm in Englewood, New Jersey.
1906–7	Lives in New York. Works at temporary jobs, including editorial work and freelance writing for magazines. Travels to Panama in 1907 to work on canal.
1907–8	Returns to Yale and receives degree in June 1908.
1912–14	Publishes *Hike and the Aeroplane* under the pseudonym "Tom Graham." Marries Grace Livingstone Hegger in April 1914 in New York. Publishes *Our Mr. Wrenn*.
1915	Resigns position with George H. Doran Company after the publication of *The Trail of the Hawk* to become a full-time writer.

1917   Publishes *The Job* and *The Innocents*. Son Wells born.

1919   Publishes *Free Air*. His play *Hobohemia* produced in New York.

1920   *Main Street* published.

1921–22 Begins to lecture. Travels to Europe to write *Babbitt*, which is published in 1922.

1923   Travels with Paul de Kruif, collecting material to write *Arrowsmith*. Writes *Arrowsmith* in France, revises it in London.

1924–25 Returns to the United States. Publishes *Arrowsmith*.

1926   Publishes *Mantrap*. Researches *Elmer Gantry*. Refuses Pulitzer Prize. Father dies.

1927   *Elmer Gantry* published. Returns to Europe and completes *The Man Who Knew Coolidge*.

1928   Publishes *The Man Who Knew Coolidge*. Divorces wife and marries Dorothy Thompson one month later. Returns to the U.S. and finishes *Dodsworth*.

1929   *Dodsworth* published.

1930   Second son born. Lewis awarded Nobel Prize.

1933   *Ann Vickers* published.

1934   Publishes *Work of Art* and assists in the dramatization of *Dodsworth*. *Jayhawker*, a play, produced in New York.

1935   Publishes *Selected Short Stories* and *It Can't Happen Here*. Elected to membership in the National Institute of Arts and Letters.

1936   Yale confers an honorary degree on Lewis. The Federal Theater Project produces *It Can't Happen Here*.

1938   Publishes *The Prodigal Parents* and contributes weekly book columns for *Newsweek*. Acts in lead role of touring production of *Angela Is Twenty-Two*.

1940   Publishes *Bethel Merriday* and teaches writing class at the University of Wisconsin.

1942–43 Divorces second wife. Publishes *Gideon Planish*.

1944–45 Son Wells killed in Alsace. Publishes *Cass Timberlane* and contributes monthly book reviews to *Esquire*.

1947   *Kingsblood Royal* published.

1949   Publishes *The God-Seeker* and sails for Italy.

1951   Dies in Rome on January 10 of heart disease. Ashes returned to Sauk Centre. *World So Wide* published posthumously.

Contributors

HAROLD BLOOM, Sterling Professor of the Humanities at Yale University, is the author of *The Anxiety of Influence*, *Poetry and Repression*, and many other volumes of literary criticism. His forthcoming study, *Freud: Transference and Authority*, attempts a full-scale reading of all of Freud's major writings. A MacArthur Prize Fellow, he is general editor of five series of literary criticism published by Chelsea House.

H. L. MENCKEN was one of the foremost literary critics and newspapermen of the 1920s, 30s, and 40s. In addition to serving as editor of the *Baltimore Evening Sun*, he wrote *The American Language*, *The Philosophy of Friedrich Nietzsche*, and *George Bernard Shaw: His Plays*. His essays and reminiscences are collected in his *Prejudices* series, *Newspaper Days* and *Heathen Days*.

T. K. WHIPPLE taught at the University of California at Berkeley. He was the author of *Martial and the English Epigram from Sir Thomas Wyatt to Ben Jonson*, and essays on Henry Adams, Theodore Dreiser, Robert Frost, and Carl Sandburg.

MARK SCHORER is a biographer of Lewis and D. H. Lawrence, editor of several anthologies, and author of a novel and a collection of short stories, *The State of Mind*.

CHARLES E. ROSENBERG is Professor of History at the University of Pennsylvania. He is the author of *The Cholera Years: The U.S. in 1832, 1849, and 1866*, *The Trial of Assassin Guiteau*, the editor of *Healing and History*, and has published essays on the history of American science and American social and intellectual history.

DANIEL R. BROWN is Lecturer in English at the State University of California, Fresno.

MARTIN BUCCO, Professor of English at Colorado State University, is the author of works on *An American Tragedy* and has written for Twayne's *World Authors Series* on Wilbur Daniel Steele and René Wellek.

STEPHEN S. CONROY is Associate Professor of History at the University of Florida and the author of essays on Emerson, Veblen, and Lewis as well as other works on American popular culture.

HOWELL DANIELS is Secretary of the Institute of United States Studies at the University of London and has published numerous essays on American literature.

NAN BAUER MAGLIN is Assistant Professor of English at Manhattan Community College. She is the author of "Images of Women in Literature," and has published essays in *Michigan Papers in Women's Studies, Prospects*, and *Radical Teacher*.

MARTIN LIGHT is Professor of English at Purdue University and has coauthored *Critical Approaches to American Literature* and *The World of Words: A Language Reader*. He has also edited *Studies in Babbitt* and written essays on Hemingway and Lewis.

Bibliography

Anderson, David, ed. *MidAmerica III*. East Lansing: Michigan State University, Midwestern Press, 1977.

——. *MidAmerica IV*. East Lansing: Michigan State University, Midwestern Press, 1977.

Austin, Allen. "An Interview with Sinclair Lewis." *University Review* 24 (Spring 1958): 199–210.

Babcock, C. Merton. "Americanisms in the Novels of Sinclair Lewis." *American Speech* 35 (May 1960): 110–16.

Baden, A. L., ed. *To the Young Writer*. Ann Arbor: University of Michigan Press, 1965.

Bloomfield, Morton W., ed. *The Interpretation of Narrative: Theory and Practice*. Harvard English Studies, no. 1. Cambridge: Harvard University Press, 1970.

Bode, Carl, ed. *The Young Rebel in American Literature*. London: Heinemann, 1959.

Bradbury, Malcolm, and David Palmer, eds. *The American Novel and the Nineteen Twenties*. Stratford-upon-Avon Studies, no. 13. London: Edward Arnold, 1971.

Carpenter, Frederick I. "Sinclair Lewis and the Fortress of Reality." *College English* 16 (April 1955): 416–23.

Clark, Walter H., Jr. "Aspects of Tragedy in *Babbitt*." *Michigan Academician* 8 (Winter 1976) 277–85.

Coard, Robert L. "Names in the Fiction of Sinclair Lewis." *The Georgia Review* 16 (Fall 1962): 318–29.

——. "Sinclair Lewis's *Kingsblood Royal*: A Thesis Novel for the Forties." *Sinclair Lewis Newsletter* 7–8 (1975–76): 10–17.

Cohen, Hennig, ed. *Landmarks of American Writing*. New York: Basic Books, 1969.

Couch, William, Jr. "Sinclair Lewis: Crisis in the American Dream." *CLA Journal* 7 (March 1964): 224–34.

Cowley, Malcolm, ed. *After the Genteel Tradition*. New York: Norton, 1937.

DeVoto, Bernard. *The Literary Fallacy*. Boston: Little, Brown, 1944.

Dooley, David Joseph. *The Art of Sinclair Lewis*. Lincoln: University of Nebraska Press, 1967.

Douglas, George H. "*Main Street* after Fifty Years." *The Prairie Schooner* 44, no. 4 (Winter 1970–71): 338–48.

Fife, Jim L. "Two Views of the American West." *Western American Literature* 1 (Spring 1966): 34–43.

Flanagan, John T. "A Long Way to Gopher Prairie: Sinclair Lewis's Apprenticeship." *Southwest Review* 32 (Autumn 1947): 403–13.

———. "The Minnesota Backgrounds of Sinclair Lewis's Fiction." *Minnesota History* 37 (March 1960): 1–13.

Fleissner, Robert F. "L'Affaire Sinclair Lewis: 'Anti-Semitism?' and Ancillary Matters." *Sinclair Lewis Newsletter* 4 (Spring 1972): 14–16.

———. " 'Something out of Dickens' in Sinclair Lewis." *Bulletin of the New York Public Library* 74 (November 1970): 607–16.

French, Warren G., and Walter E. Kidd, eds. *American Winners of the Nobel Literary Prize*. Norman: University of Oklahoma Press, 1968.

Fyvel, T. R. "Martin Arrowsmith and His Habitat." *The New Republic*, 18 July 1955, 16–18.

Gardiner, Harold C., ed. *Fifty Years of the American Novel*. New York: Scribner's, 1952.

Gauss, Christian. "Sinclair Lewis vs. His Education." *The Saturday Evening Post*, 26 December 1931, 19–21, 54–56.

Geismar, Maxwell. *American Moderns: From Rebellion to Conformity*. New York: Hill & Wang, 1958.

———. *The Last of the Provincials: The American Novel 1915–1925*. Boston: Houghton Mifflin, 1947.

Grebstein, Sheldon. "The Education of a Rebel: Sinclair Lewis at Yale." *New England Quarterly* 28 (September 1955): 377–82.

———. *Sinclair Lewis*. New York: Twayne, 1962.

———. "Sinclair Lewis and the Nobel Prize." *Western Humanities Review* 13 (Spring 1959): 163–71.

Griffin, Robert J., ed. *Twentieth Century Interpretations of* Arrowsmith. Englewood Cliffs, N.J.: Prentice-Hall, 1968.

Hassan, Ihab. *Radical Innocence: The Contemporary American Novel*. Princeton: Princeton University Press, 1961.

Helleberg, Marilyn M. "The Paper-Doll Characters of Sinclair Lewis's *Arrowsmith*." *Mark Twain Journal* 14 (1969): 17–21.

Hilfer, Anthony Channell. *The Revolt from the Village*. Chapel Hill: University of North Carolina Press, 1969.

Hoffman, Frederick J. *The Twenties: American Writing in the Postwar Decade*. New York: Viking, 1955.

Hunt, Frazier. *One American and His Attempt at Education*. New York: Simon & Schuster, 1938.

Kazin, Alfred. *On Native Grounds: An Interpretation of Modern American Prose Literature*. New York: Reynal & Hitchcock, 1942.

Lewis, Robert W. "*Babbitt* and the Dream of Romance." *North Dakota Quarterly* 40, no. 1 (Winter 1972): 7–14.

Light, Martin. "Lewis's Finicky Girls and Faithful Workers." *University Review* 30 (Winter 1963): 151–59.

———. *The Quixotic Vision of Sinclair Lewis*. West Lafayette, Ind.: Purdue University Press, 1975.

———. *Studies in* Babbitt. Columbus, Ohio: Merrill, 1970.

Lundquist, James. *Guide to Sinclair Lewis*. Columbus, Ohio: Merrill, 1971.

————. *Sinclair Lewis*. New York: Frederick Ungar, 1973.

Maddon, David, ed. *American Dreams and American Nightmares*. Carbondale: Southern Illinois University Press, 1970.

Manfred, Frederick F. "Sinclair Lewis: A Portrait." *American Scholar* 23 (Spring 1954): 162–84.

Millgate, Michael. *American Social Fiction, James to Cozzens*. Edinburgh: Oliver & Boyd, 1964.

Petrullo, Helen B. *"Babbitt* as Situational Satire." *Kansas Quarterly* 1 (Summer 1969): 89–97.

————. *"Main Street, Cass Timberlane*, and Determinism." *South Dakota Review* 7, no. 4 (Winter 1969–70): 30–42.

Quivey, James R. "George Babbitt's Quest for Masculinity." *Ball State University Forum* 10, no. 2 (Spring 1969): 4–7.

Richardson, Lyon N. *"Arrowsmith:* Genesis, Development, Versions." *American Literature* 27 (May 1955): 225–44.

Schorer, Mark. "The Monstrous Self-Deception of Elmer Gantry." *The New Republic*, 31 October 1955, 13–15.

————. *Sinclair Lewis*. Minneapolis: University of Minnesota Press, 1963.

————. *Society and Self in the Novel*. English Institute Essays. New York: Columbia University Press, 1955.

————. *Sinclair Lewis. A Collection of Critical Essays*. Englewood Cliffs, N.J.: Prentice-Hall, 1962.

Sherman, Stuart P. *The Significance of Sinclair Lewis*. New York: Harcourt, Brace & World, 1922.

Sinclair Lewis Newsletter. St. Cloud, Minn.: St. Cloud State College, 1969–.

Stegner, Wallace, ed. *The American Novel*. New York: Basic Books, 1965.

Tepperman, Jay. "The Research Scientist in Modern Fiction." *Perspectives in Biology and Medicine* 3 (1960): 550–53.

Thorp, Willard. *American Writing in the Twentieth Century*. Cambridge: Harvard University Press, 1960.

Tuttleton, James W. *The Novel of Manners in America*. Chapel Hill: University of North Carolina Press, 1972.

Wagenaar, Dick. "The Knight and the Pioneer: Europe and America in the Fiction of Sinclair Lewis." *American Literature* 50 (May 1978): 230–49.

West, Rebecca. *The Strange Necessity*. New York: Doubleday, 1928.

Whipple, T. K. *Spokesmen*. New York: D. Appleton, 1928.

Yoshida, Hiroshige. *A Sinclair Lewis Lexicon with a Critical Study of His Style and Method*. Tokyo: Hoyu Press, 1976.

Acknowledgments

"Portrait of an American Citizen" by H. L. Mencken from *Sinclair Lewis: A Collection of Critical Essays*, edited by Mark Schorer, © 1962 by the Enoch Pratt Free Library. Reprinted by permission of the Enoch Pratt Free Library in accordance with the terms of the will of H. L. Mencken.

"Glass Flowers, Waxworks, and the Barnyard Symphonies of Sinclair Lewis" (originally entitled "Sinclair Lewis") by T. K. Whipple from *Spokesman: Modern Writers and American Life* by T. K. Whipple, © 1928 by E. P. Dutton. Reprinted by permission. Excerpt from *Babbitt* by Sinclair Lewis, © 1922 by Harcourt Brace Jovanovich, Inc.; renewed 1950 by Sinclair Lewis. Reprinted by permission of Harcourt Brace Jovanovich, Inc. and Jonathan Cape, Ltd.

"Sinclair Lewis and the Method of Half-Truths" by Mark Schorer from *Sinclair Lewis: A Collection of Critical Essays*, edited by Mark Schorer, © 1962 by Mark Schorer. Reprinted by permission of Prentice-Hall, Inc., Englewood Cliffs, New Jersey.

"Martin Arrowsmith: The Scientist as Hero" by Charles E. Rosenberg from *American Quarterly* 15, no. 3 (Fall 1963), © 1963 by the Trustees of the University of Pennsylvania. Reprinted by permission of the author and *American Quarterly*.

"Lewis's Satire—A Negative Emphasis" by Daniel R. Brown from *Renascence: Essays on Values in Literature* 18, no. 2 (Winter 1966), © 1966 by the Catholic Renascence Society, Inc. Reprinted by permission of *Renascence: Essays on Values in Literature*.

"The Serialized Novels of Sinclair Lewis" by Martin Bucco from *Western American Literature* 4, no. 1 (Spring 1969), © 1969 by the Western Literature Association. Reprinted by permission.

"Sinclair Lewis's Sociological Imagination" by Stephen S. Conroy from *American Literature* 42, no. 3 (November 1970), © 1970 by Duke University Press. Reprinted by permission.

"Sinclair Lewis and the Drama of Dissociation" by Howell Daniels from *The American Novel and the Nineteen Twenties* (Stratford upon Avon Studies 13), edited by Malcolm Bradbury and David Palmer, © 1971 by Edward Arnold (Publishers) Ltd. Reprinted by permission.

"Women in Three Sinclair Lewis Novels" by Nan Bauer Maglin from *The Massachusetts Review* 14, no. 4 (Autumn 1973), © 1974 by The Massachusetts Review, Inc. Reprinted by permission.

"Dodsworth: The Quixotic Hero" (originally entitled "Dodsworth") by Martin Light from *The Quixotic Vision of Sinclair Lewis* by Martin Light, © 1975 by the Purdue Research Foundation. Reprinted by permission of the Purdue Research Foundation, West Lafayette, Indiana. All rights reserved.

Index

Addams, Jane, 113
Alice Adams (Tarkington), 109
American Tragedy, An (Dreiser), 4
"America the Beautiful" (McCarthy),
 86
Anatomy of Satire, The (Highet), 60
Anderson, Sherwood, 21, 31, 83, 97
Animal Farm (Orwell), 52
Ann Vickers, 103–18, 115–17; East vs.
 West theme in, 67; as edited for
 publication in Redbook, 64–65,
 65–66, 67; feminist movement in,
 115, 116; marriage vs. work
 conflict in, 106; serialized version
 of, 64; sexual content of, 66;
 socialist movement in, 115; style
 of, 59; women in, 106, 115, 118;
 women's suffrage movement in,
 106, 116, 117. *See also individual
 characters*
Anthony, Susan B., 106
Appleby, Mother (*The Innocents*), 69
Arrowsmith, 21, 41–50, 61, 82, 100;
 alienation in, 72, 77; caricature in,
 2; children in, 78; despair in, 78;
 East vs. West theme in, 67; as
 edited for publication in serial
 form, 65, 67; individual vs. society
 in, 78; isolation in, 77; League of
 Cultural Agencies in, 49; male
 chauvinism in, 85; materialism in,
 41, 77; medicine in, 42–50;
 optimism in, 77; as romance, 2;
 satire in, 2; science in, 2, 42–50;
 science idealized in, 2, 3; science
 vs. worldly success in, 76;
 serialized version of, 64, 65, 67;

social conflict in, 77; sources of,
 43–50; theme of, 101; title of, 45;
 weaknesses in plot of, 77;
 withdrawal from society in, 78;
 women in, 85. *See also individual
 characters*
Arrowsmith, Leora (*Arrowsmith*), 17,
 20–21; death of, 77
Arrowsmith, Martin (*Arrowsmith*), 21,
 30, 91; as an American, 2; as a
 hero, 41, 126; integrity of, 11, 41;
 rejection of society of, 50; science
 vs. worldly success in, 76; sense of
 beauty of, 53; as Sinclair Lewis, 2;
 social inadequacies of, 50; sources
 for, 43–50
Awakening, The (Chopin), 112
Azeredo, Nande (*Dodsworth*), 98,
 123–24

Babbitt, 61, 66, 91–97, 100; adjustment
 in, 72, 76; ambivalence toward
 subject matter in, 53; American
 society in, 7; apathy in, 11;
 character development in, 6, 91;
 childhood in, 95; children in, 76,
 78; compared to *Main Street*, 5, 73,
 92–93; compared to *The Prodigal
 Parents*, 56; conformity in, 76, 82;
 dissociation in, 87, 94; dreams in,
 95; fantasy in, 93; hatred in, 52;
 hope in, 76; humor in, 96;
 hyperbole in, 95, 96; individual vs.
 society in, 78; irony in, 6, 93; life
 dehumanized in, 11; Walter
 Lippmann's comments on, 56;